THE GREATER MAN

THE GREATER MAN

Anirudh Garg

NEW DEGREE PRESS

COPYRIGHT © 2022 ANIRUDH GARG

THE GREATER MAN

ISBN

979-8-88504-507-0   *Paperback*

979-8-88504-609-1   *Kindle Ebook*

979-8-88504-159-1   *Digital Ebook*

To my father Kelpesh Garg and my grandfather M. S. Narayan,
for teaching me the differences between a boy and a man.

CONTENTS

INTRODUCTION

To start this book, I must be perfectly clear: women are better than men. In the modern world with changing needs and new horizons, women have the superior temperament and skillsets to succeed. I passionately believe if institutionalized sexism disappeared from the face of the earth, men would only have an edge on women in athleticism, and maybe comedy.

Feminist writer Julie Bindel in a 2017 op-ed in the *Guardian* phrases it eloquently. She notes according to the *British Medical Journal*, "women make better surgeons than their male counterparts, and that 4% fewer patients die following an operation performed by a woman." In addition, women might be better entrepreneurs because "women are consistently more successful than men in reaching funding targets for crowdfunding projects." Girls are also much better students. Boys used to have a slight lead in math and science, but those advantages have all but closed (Crawford, 2019). Now, women stand as the more academically gifted sex on average.

These victories from women weren't inherited, they were earned. Women have had to climb an uphill battle for the last three centuries for their right to be valid in every facet of society. British public schools in the 1920s discouraged girls "from being 'over-conscientious' and putting their reproductive organs at risk" (Kuper, 2018). Feminism has made great strides in the empowerment of women, from suffrage to paid maternity leave. As the conditions for women gets better, I push for men to invest in themselves and the project of masculinity to stay competitive and cooperative with women.

To those who kept reading after my controversial take, I commend you. Reading this book requires the resolve to swallow hard truths. We need to challenge misconceptions and delusions that have been indoctrinated into all of us. The first step to fixing a problem is admitting there is one in the first place. This book starts with admitting the problem with masculinity.

There is a crisis of masculinity across the globe, and its fundamental problem draws from the question, "What is the role of men in the modern world?" Young men get a lot of mixed messages on what is expected of them. They look at stories of billionaires like Elon Musk, athletes like LeBron James, or actors like Channing Tatum and believe those are the pinnacles of manhood. Growing up is hard enough as is, but if the definition for a healthy and successful man changes every time Hollywood casts a new James Bond, then it bears no surprise misguided young men morph into destructive criminals or isolated and depressed underachievers.

Positive masculine role models blessed my formative years. As an admittedly precocious child, I spent most of my interactions with adults learning from their wisdom. I spent a lot of time at family gatherings near the adult's table learning about business and politics. Eventually, with more than a little help from the internet, I began contributing to those discussions. Instead of being shut down or ignored, I was elevated to a level of importance. That dynamic inspired me to pass on wisdom to children younger than me. My first job was tutoring, and afterward most of my volunteering experience has included helping struggling kids. I understand what it's like to be the strange and awkward kid in school. Understanding that awkward adolescent insecurity is exactly what prompted me to write this book.

I don't like the term "toxic masculinity" because it is an overly simplistic understanding of masculine needs and expression. There is a prevailing myth aggression and competition are dangerous for society, when that couldn't be further from the truth. These are parts of the human psyche. Every human—man, woman, or other—has masculine and feminine tendencies. Shutting down any part of that means denying a part of your being. We don't want out of control men wreaking havoc on society, but that shouldn't come at the cost of men's social, spiritual, or mental well-being.

I want this book to be dedicated to the project of productive masculinity. We need to create systems and incentives that channel the natural masculine energies of young men into healthy and productive outlets. Telling young men their desires and dreams are invalid doesn't open them up to revaluating their trajectory. There needs to empathy for the impulses of young men, not excuse for their failures.

Young men need positive role models, arguably, more than girls. Single parent households are much more destructive to a young man's confidence than to his sister's. In their formative years, boys are more vulnerable to negative influences and more in need of positive influences.

A productive masculinity teaches men to hold themselves accountable, to strive for a greater cause, and to break their chains. There needs to be an effort from everyone to help young men achieve these facets. Role models often come from the most unorthodox of places, and sometimes it takes an entire community of mentors to guide a young man through the most perilous times of his life.

For those reasons, this book is for everyone to read. The prime beneficiaries of these ideas are young men between the ages of eleven and twenty-one, but they are also pertinent to parents and educators who wish to touch the lives of struggling boys. Women also benefit from this book by better understanding the motivations of masculine men and to understand their own masculine side.

This book isn't law and shouldn't be treated as such. There are many nuances that will vary for people from different backgrounds and across different cultures. There is no ideal formula that balances all the necessary components of healthy masculinity. Such thinking is destructive to real growth. Instead of striving for an unattainable perfect balance, this book seeks the answer for greater stability.

This book compiles the wisdom of great men across different societies and backgrounds. Their success will be applauded, and their failures will be autopsied. This book doesn't concern itself with perfection, rather with action. Paralysis by analysis is a grave threat for uncertain and misguided youth. Just as it is easier to ask for forgiveness than permission, it's easier to move fast and break things than it is to agonize over reaching perfection on the first try. Resilience is underrated in growth. We need to create systems that encourage everyone to fail and pick themselves back up to fail again.

To young men who hesitate to start the book, I have only one thing left to say: you have nothing to lose but your chains.

CHAPTER 1

HISTORY OF MASCULINITY

———

To start this discussion on masculinity, it is pertinent this book adequately defines the concept. The dictionary will define masculinity as a man's characteristics—the most useless tautology in the world. The colloquial understanding of masculinity pounded into young boys' impressionable minds is embodied by a physically strong, socially dominant, successful, and sexually potent man.

The best example is James Bond, a devout patriot who fights international terrorists, drives fancy cars, wears expensive suits, and seduces every woman in his sight.

The problem with James Bond is his example helps no one. As a fictional character, he escapes many of the consequences of his actions, especially with how poorly he treats women. The government funds his lifestyle, and he is guaranteed to succeed no matter the crisis.

Bond's character follows the rule of cool. Still, as our society enters a new enlightenment thanks to the #MeToo and Time's Up movements, we expect more from men than hedonistic wish fulfillment. Bond is a terrible human being, and as much as I loathe the term "toxic masculinity," it applies more to him than possibly any other modern character.

The term "toxic masculinity" does an abysmal job of addressing a genuine problem with the crisis of masculinity. It is vital we remain critical of all social conventions. We can only innovate once we understand the flaws within the current model.

"Toxic masculinity" does not offer a critique beyond certain behaviors being bad. For many despondent young men, that is not a convincing argument to change their entire worldview. Certainly not when decades of media and culture condition them otherwise.

Discourse around masculinity needs a positive model to contrast with traditional masculinity, a model where good faith criticism meets genuine and effective solutions. Criticism without solutions is just whining and that is not an effective model to change the behaviors of young men.

The issue with our understanding of masculinity is our inability to socialize young boys. American political scientist and author of *The Myth of Male Power* Warren Farrell points out the issue with socialization: "If our very survival has been dependent on our sons' willingness to die, being sensitive to male death competes with our survival instinct."

Patriarchy asks men to sacrifice their lives in armed conflicts. In a sinking ship, they are the last priority. Treating male mortality callously has negative consequences to society.

A longitudinal study on teenage suicidality found that "between 1975 and 2016, a total of 85,051 suicide deaths were identified for youth aged 10 to 19 years in the United States (68,085 male [80.1%] and 16,966 female [19.9%])" (Ruch, 2019). Young boys are far more likely to commit suicide because they are more likely to face social isolation and mental health breakdowns.

A meta-analysis from 2019 notes "both the objective condition of being alone (e.g., living alone) and the subjective feeling of being alone (i.e., loneliness) were strongly associated with suicidal outcomes," and these findings crossed all cultures (Hall-Lande, 2007).

Without a proper guide for socialization, young men will not find their place in a changing society. Masculinity is gravely needed to socialize and develop young boys into men.

Michael Salter at the *Atlantic*, when interviewing sociologist Raewyn Connell, notes the failures of men should be viewed as the "product of relations and behaviors, rather than as a fixed set of identities and attributes." Both Salter and Connell understand that solutions for resolving the crisis of masculinity should index "the situations in which groups of men act, the patterns in their actions, and the consequences of what they do" (Salter, 2020).

This book is not interested in politicizing the issue of masculinity. That opens the door to grifters and con artists. I care far more for improving the material conditions of young men. My understanding of masculinity centers itself on empowering young men to be the best versions of themselves and inspiring other men to do the same.

My definition is masculinity embodies the traits of being reliable and accountable to the people in your life, being driven for a cause, and having broken your chains. I believe adhering to these principles begins the arduous task of becoming a real man who uplifts himself and those around him in the pursuit of a better world.

Masculinity is in crisis because the meaning of being a man has completely changed. We no longer live in a world where a man must provide for his family as the sole breadwinner or be the one to bear the costs of war. Largely, this change has benefited both men and women.

Unfortunately, many young men have not been socialized to maximize their newfound fortune. While women's empowerment has made strides in creating gender parity, men's liberation has not been as successful. Many young men are lost because they cannot follow the same life path as their fathers and are fearful they will not share the same prosperity.

There are a dangerous multitude of grifters answering that call for help with harmful and destructive ideas. Young men, filled with anxiety and bereft of direction, have a dangerous susceptibility to radicalization—political or religious—and may harm themselves and others.

In response to the dangers of harmful masculinity, there have been pushes to blame the harm done by men on masculinity at large, and I cannot disagree with that sentiment. It is men who lack a productive and healthy masculinity who are responsible for the violence and destruction caused by men. A healthy understanding of masculinity will ameliorate these societal ills.

While it is true men commit far more violent crime than women, a large portion of that has to do with a failure on the part of men in controlling and productively channeling their darker impulses. This book aims to turn the weaknesses and threats associated with men into strengths and opportunities.

The alcohol industry would like you to believe toxic masculinity is responsible for all domestic violence in the world. Unfortunately, the empirical evidence casts a spotlight on their bloody hands. A meta-analysis on alcohol and its relationship with intimate partner violence found "an increase of 10 alcohol outlets per 10,000 persons was associated with 34% increase in male-to-female partner violence" (Targum, 2012).

Alcohol has always been a social lubricant and media has always portrayed the hero of many stories as a smooth drinker who spreads merriment or intrigue between sips. The alcohol industry markets its product as the magic substance to bring good times and good company.

Alcohol is a very telling indicator for a failure to adhere to the masculine goals. Those who abuse alcohol have their ability to care for their family diminished, sometimes to the point of being violent with them. Alcohol abuse also kills a man's inherent drive to succeed, leaving him in a state of limbo where he constantly looks forward to the next glass. Alcohol is a vice and hangs on the chains of many men, robbing them of their strengths and feeding their weaknesses.

Alcohol isn't inherently evil, but understanding how it feeds into the destruction of healthy masculinity is imperative. I personally enjoy alcohol, but I follow strict rules in its consumption so I don't cross the line from use to abuse. I only drink in safe social gatherings and use alcohol as a social lubricant. I don't rely on it to socialize, but I enjoy its relaxing properties. I never turn to the bottle when I am stressed, upset, or angry because that sets a dangerous precedent.

The reason why this book addresses men directly is because men and women are different. Aside from sexual dimorphism, which is visually apparent, there are big differences in the behaviors of men and women.

The masculine nature of Japanese society places a massive burden on young men, such as the workaholic culture and the importance of collectivist cultural values. It punishes free thinking and disagreeable men. Men are under great stress to meet societal expectations. In a 2012 analysis of overwork-related suicide, Junko Kitanaka, PhD, a medical anthropologist trained at the University of Chicago, explains "Japan has the third highest rate of annual suicide (after Hungary) and has witnessed a staggering 30,000 deaths per year for the past decade related in part to the sustained economic recession." Men who fail to meet the standards for masculinity feel cast out, and in their desperation after losing their job or failing to support their families cast their violence inward. Men are 2.3 times more likely to commit suicide than women according to the Japanese Ministry of Health, and it is the leading cause of death for men between fifteen and forty-nine years old (Semuels, 2017).

Another area where men have different outcomes in their behavior is in the American education system. A Stanford educational analysis from 2018 has uncovered changing trends in K–12 education. Historically, girls tended to out-perform boys in reading and writing standardized test scores, whereas boys held an advantage in math and science. However, since 2018, girls have outpaced boys in improvement across the board. The lead girls have in reading and writing have increased and the gaps in math and science have shrunk. In poorer school districts, girls tend to outperform boys in math and science (Barbee, 2017).

Pedagogical changes over the past forty years in American education are partly responsible for the rise in test scores in girls. The switch from teacher-focused learning to student-fo-cused learning has had profound impacts on children. Instead of strict authoritarian discipline from the teacher, allowing children to learn through discovery has helped children learn at a much faster pace in formative years. Unfortunately, gains from the changes in pedagogy aren't uniform. While boys and girls have both benefitted, girls benefit much more.

The difference becomes much more significant as boys and girls get ready for college. Alana Semuels, when writing for the *Atlantic*, notes, "This gender gap in college completion has been a long time in the making. In the early 1900s, when some elite colleges started opening up to women, women quickly got better grades than men" (Ruch, 2019). In 1967, 57 percent of male high school grads attended college, far more than the

47 percent of women. However, it is expected by 2024 over 57 percent of college graduates will be women. That translates to over 3.2 million more women graduating in raw numbers over men. The jump in woman's higher education participation comes from women from low-income backgrounds who are leaving behind their brothers. "How parents raise children can exacerbate these dynamics. Pressures to be 'masculine' are often stronger in lower-income or working-class families," notes Claudia Buchmann, a professor of sociology at Ohio State. "The notion of what it means to be a boy and a man, especially among lower working-class boys, makes it such that they see doing well in school as something that girls and women do, and they don't want any part of it."

As many traditionally masculine jobs like coal mining and even truck driving slowly fade away due to changes in the structure of the US economy, job opportunities for less educated men will shrink. If jobs requiring an education don't appeal to a boy's sense of masculinity, they are less invested in their educational outcomes.

Buchamn further explains "students who reported getting mostly As in middle school have a 70 percent chance of completing college by age 25, while those who get mostly Cs have only a 10 percent chance" (Semuels, 2017). This is deeply worrying in a society where more and more jobs require a college degree.

The notion women are better suited for the modern world holds true even in developing countries. In Zimbabwe, there is an all-women park ranger squad whose goal is to stop poachers from killing animals in wildlife sanctuaries. This is a fascinating phenomenon because this is not a stereotypically feminine profession, and I find this hilarious because these women tend to be much, much more effective than their male counterparts (IFC, 2012).

One reason why they are credited for their efficacy in comparison to male rangers is because they drink a lot less. They tend to be more focused on their job, suffer from fewer distractions, and put in more work in training. This holds true in expansive public policy. An IFC jobs study found there is a significant difference in the spending habits of men and women: "Research suggests that women-headed households reinvest 90 percent of their income into their families, compared to 30 to 40 percent contributed by men." This means women are more likely to provide medical care, robust nutrition, and education for their children than men.

If the foundational building blocks of society are family, it appears women build stronger families and therefore more robust societies. One of the reasons why men are less interested in the project of family building is because of their weakness to vices. Men are more susceptible to drinking away their paycheck or gambling away their savings (IFC, 2012). The inclination to vice is not a moral failing. If there aren't productive institutions and motivations in a society, vices become more appealing. People who feel as though their life has no direction or meaning find distractions attractive.

Masculinity is about showcasing the best aspects of a man. Men who are masculine provide significant contributions to humanity. We need to acknowledge the project of masculinity is a perpetual struggle against the demons holding men back. When men are young, they are the weakest to those demons. Bulldozing all sins in society never works. You can ban drugs, but mafias and cartels take over the streets. You can moralize pornography and sex work, but those will just become money makers for human traffickers.

There is an instinct to ban or shame illness in public policy. The crack epidemic of the 1980s and 1990s was met with the full force of criminal justice systems rather than any public health apparatuses. Masculinity cannot afford such treatment. Feminizing men isn't the solution because it will be met with pushback. Many men will resent this idea for purely aesthetic reasons.

The Alternative Right, Men's Rights Activists, and involuntary celibates (incels) are just symptoms of a society that has a poor relationship with masculinity. When you get rid of Sean Connery but don't give young men an inspirational paradigm, they will refuse to listen to you. Getting rid of masculinity sets a dangerous precedent because it seeks to solve problems by a politics of division.

Everyone, gender aside, has a masculine side and a feminine side. Men tend to be more masculine and women tend to be more feminine. These concepts may be the product of evolutionary biology or social conditioning, but that doesn't change they are a part of people.

Telling men that behaving in a feminine manner will fix their problems is the same as telling a Jewish person they can be free of anti-Semitism by adopting the quintessential WASP (White Anglo-Saxon Protestant) lifestyle. You are asking them to sunder their heritage rather than help them preserve and innovate on top of their identity.

Most men want to be masculine and a few women want to as well. If they are going to develop a relationship with masculinity they need every helpful tool they can get.

If you peruse Amazon's catalog with a query for women's empowerment, you will receive over five hundred different book recommendations for girls in STEM alone. Similar prescriptions for men don't exist because they don't need to. Men are overwhelmingly represented in positions of power and influence.

The material conditions of young men are the result of poor socialization. Men need liberation, empowerment from harmful expectations. The liberation of men is not the oppression of women, it is their empowerment. Insecure and destructive men hurt women. This book is interested in the liberation of men because the patriarchal norms that harm women also harm men.

For a boy to become a man, he needs ways to fulfill his physical, emotional, psychological, financial, and spiritual needs. The way this book aims to materially make progress toward these needs is by giving young men the framework to build a fulfilling life through masculinity. The reason why I define a healthy masculinity as one that builds systems that hold men accountable to the people around them, that pushes them to pursue a higher cause, and that sunders their chains, is because I believe the meaningful pursuit of these goals give an immediate and material improvement in well-being.

The overworked and lonely salaryman in Japan, the American high-school dropout who fell in with the wrong crowd, and the young man in a developing country getting his first job are all facing the same exact question. What kind of man should I be? It is a difficult question and we shouldn't judge those who don't immediately have a perfect answer. We should encourage them to keep an open mind and build better systems in their life to lift them out of their struggles.

CHAPTER 2

PILLARS OF THE COMMUNITY

———

One of the most formative stories I heard growing up was the story of Ekalavya. In the *Mahabharata*, an Indian epic, there is a great war fought for the kingdom of Hastinapur in Northern India. Ekalavya was the son of a minor bureaucrat with dreams of mastering archery. His family could not afford a teacher, so he made his bow from twigs and hair and practiced in front of the statue of the most legendary teacher in all of ancient India, Dronacharya.

Anytime he hit a roadblock he would spy on Guru Drona as he taught the young princes of Hastinapur and imitate all he learned. One day a loud dog interrupted his training with its incessant barking. Not wanting to hurt the animal, Ekalavya fired his arrows into the dog's maw in a geometric arrangement that prevented him from barking. When the young princes found the dog sometime later, they tracked down Ekalavya out of curiosity and introduced him to their teacher.

Drona was shaken to the core. He had promised one of the princes, Arjun, he would become the greatest archer in all the lands, but a low-born child with no formal training had eclipsed both of them. A common virtue of heroes in Hindu scripture was their drive to fulfill their oaths (Arjun's older brother Yudhisthira once forced all four of his younger brothers into slavery after losing a bet). Dronacharya, wanting to keep his vow to Arjun, asked for Guru Dakshina, a payment for teachings. He argued because Ekalavya had spied, he had taken his education dishonorably.

Ekalavya, with great earnestness, got on his knees and asked how he could pay the Guru Dakshina, for he had no wealth. Drona, seizing the opportunity, asked for his right thumb as compensation. Ekalavya severed his thumb and presented it before Drona. With Ekalavya's draw-hand crippled Drona knew he could mold Arjun into the greatest archer who ever lived, or so he thought.

Years later, when both Drona and Ekalavya found each other on opposite sides of a war, Drona was shocked once more. Ekalavya had learned to fire arrows with his left hand with skill that transcended what he had displayed in his youth. Drona fell by Ekalavya's arrows and paid the price for his hubris. But when the war ended, Ekalavya humbled himself before the funeral pyre of his former teacher and thanked him for all he learned.

The story of Ekalavya taught me an important lesson best conveyed by the Sanskrit saying, "Matha, Pitha, Guru, Devam." After any success, a man must thank his mother, father, teachers, and the higher power. Ekalavya taught me to stay mindful of all the people who helped me succeed in life. I would not be alive if my parents didn't take care of me. I wouldn't feel confident enough to write this book without the wisdom and encouragement of my mentors. I personally don't believe in a higher power, but I recognize a person's faith and religious community also abuts their triumphs. This is not a lesson we can escape; there is no self-made man.

One of the most ridiculous labels a successful person can give themselves is the moniker of the "Self-Made Man." No human is born by themselves; they had someone who carried them in the womb for nine months, a team of doctors, nurses, or midwives aiding in their delivery, and a whole village to raise them. We are incredibly malleable beings, and our environment affects us.

The role masculinity plays in social spaces is pivotal to their survival. Men must learn to work together to accomplish shared goals for the good of their community. Masculinity provides the energy to find creative solutions, invest the time in mastering their process, and cooperating to get them accomplished. Men who don't engage in their social spaces will find it harder to live a healthy life.

A Wisconsin longitudinal study on male volunteers found "continuous volunteering for a variety of organizations appears to lead to more positive effects on psychological well-being. Working for three or more types of organizations provided more benefit than working for two, which had more effect than working for one or none" (Piliavin 2007). These benefits also had a much stronger return on investment with men who suffered from anti-social tendencies because "the relationship of volunteering to psychological well-being is moderated by level of social integration, with those who are less well integrated benefiting the most."

Volunteering connects men to their communities and social institutions. As they help others, they help themselves overcome their own isolation. It is an incredibly powerful activity, but there are other ways young men can invest in their community.

Economists have a cornucopia of data to demonstrate the benefit in investing in strong social institutions. The most basic unit of human cooperation is family and the social institution of marriage is the traditional starting point of a family.

Men who invest in marriage receive a wage premium. "Cross-sectional analysis yields a wage premium for married men of about 15 percent." These "results are consistent with the hypothesis that employers use marriage as a signal–a large proportion of the marriage premium is due to unobservable characteristics that are valued both by wives and by employers, such as motivation, loyalty, dependability and determination" (Bardasi 2005). Marriage is another way men are tied to their community. When a man's interests overlap with the community's he will always find a helping hand, even a silent one.

Community is a vital tool for the creation of better men. Other people offer their wisdom and expertise. Every generation builds on the foundation laid by previous generations.

It's crucial we respect our elders. Baby Boomers get a bad reputation, but they have lived longer lives than younger generations. They made incalculable mistakes regarding the environment, public policy, housing, fashion, education, even romantic partners. But those mistakes are powerful tools for learning and the burden placed on younger generations is to learn from the mistakes of the past to build a better future. It is not masculine to disregard wisdom, no matter the source.

Wisdom can be learned in two ways, through the example of others or through personal experience. There are certain things we can learn as outside observers: issues of economics, policy, and science. Unfortunately, there are many more we can't learn without an intimate understanding of human biases.

The best argument for respecting your elders is to gain their mentorship. It is intimidating to undertake a new venture. It does not matter if it's a new career path, college major, sport, or even learning an instrument. Whenever we try something new, we encounter a learning curve. Sometimes we can grit our teeth and bang against it to learn a new skill, but that's the most wasteful strategy. The best method is by finding a mentor.

There are a plethora of different options and decisions you can take. You might have a long-term goal, but that is useless if you cannot see the path two steps ahead of you. A mentor is a person who understands the intricacies of their field and can warn you of any pitfalls, because they were ensnared by those same obstacles.

Mentors are crucial to building on the works of the past. Many great scientists created their magnum opus off the back of their mentors and inspiration. Science is the enterprise of replacing error with ignorance. In any field, we accept the greatest mysteries are restricted to us by our own limited understanding, technology, and resources. Einstein theorized the existence of a particle that gave all matter mass, but his ideas outlived him. In 2012, scientists at CERN discovered the Higgs particle. Some of Albert Einstein's predictions were wrong, but his research still paved the way for his students and their students to build on his work. Mentorship is an important part of the scientific community and, likewise, every community.

Mentorship is not always clear cut. Ekalavaya did not have the traditional apprenticeship Arjuna had under Drona, but like the scientists who studied Einstein's papers, he built a foundation for further mastery.

A study tracking African American males in urban environments found the importance of having a male role model. The paper found "that the absence of a male role model magnifies the negative effects of peer problem behavior on adolescent problem behavior" (Bryant 2003). All male role models from fathers, uncles, brothers, and even extend family made a significant impact on positive behavior and educational outcomes.

As for how mentors outside of the family unit affected the outcome of young men, the paper found "looking up to, respecting, and viewing a family member as a role model may increase the likelihood that youth take advantage of mentoring opportunities or social capital resources that family members provide" (Bryant 2003). The research concluded that "youth who are turned off to parents and other mentors, however, lose this valuable social capital. It is likely that family members who are good role models provide positive learning environments and act as educators and advisers to youth" (Bryant 2003). Mentorship is a foundational building block for masculine engagement in communities. Without a masculine role model, many young men may not find their place in their community.

Community is an incredibly important part of the human experience, and this chapter concerns itself with utilizing masculinity to build strong communities. Masculinity asks men to protect communities, sustain them, and produce good results in doing so. There are many threats a man must stay vigilant for when building a community, with the most worrisome threats being corruption, outside actors, and neglect.

Unfortunately, one major weakness in communities with strong hierarchy is the susceptibility to corruption. Corruption is when people in power run contrary to the oath they have taken when given power. An elected representative takes the oath to serve the needs of their constituency first. The moment they betray that, they become corrupt.

There is a nuance we must understand with corruption. Promoting the interest of the group sometimes entails making harsh decisions regarding clan-based thinking. It's often seen as a moral imperative to promote people who come from your clan or tribe within your organization. Prestigious universities often weigh legacy into their admissions process. This is a harmful form of corruption for any group or institution.

Nepotism is harmful for all communities, but it is the logical consequence of a meritocracy. One of the most frustrating catch-22s of youth is the experience trap. You need experience for an entry level job, but no one will higher you because you don't have enough experience. If you open the field in the form of an internship you'll quickly be inundated by thousands of applicants without any clear-cut method to distinguish them.

Sometimes referrals and recommendations become useful tools to gauge talent. If you are unsure of a person's competence, say when hiring to fill the CEO position of a small firm, you may take the sage counsel of a trusted advisor or mentor to fill that position. There's nothing wrong with giving people a chance to prove themselves. The issue arises when you refuse to replace them should they fail to live up to your expectations.

If your boss' son oversees a team but runs every project he manages inefficiently, you have few options to fix the situation. You can't escalate it to your boss, no one wants to be told their child is incompetent. The best you could hope to do is work with the son and help him improve, but at that point, you are the leader—one who isn't getting recognized or paid for their merits.

The worst effect is even if the son proves himself to be competent enough, an underprivileged individual may never find themselves in a position to make mistakes and learn to build experience for that role. Their unique perspective would be sorely missed and important institutions will give the appearance of elitist exclusivity.

Many young men will see top schools, exclusive firms, and government positions as opulent dreams that are completely out of reach. Some will grow dejected and withdraw from society while others may stare at the garden walls in vicious envy. They may grow resentful and destructive because a child unloved by the village will burn it down to feel its warmth.

Corruption, including nepotism, weakens communities. You cannot trust the people around you—mentors, government officials, and business owners—if they don't hold your community's best interests at heart. Masculinity asks us to stand against corruption and conflicts of interest that harm communities.

A masculine landlord will ensure all his tenants live in decent and safe accommodations. When renters sign a lease, they do so for a home and a landlord has an obligation to aid in the creation of that home. A corrupt landlord will let his property fall into disrepair, endangering tenants. A masculine landlord will encourage camaraderie among his tenants, even hosting get-togethers for those living near each other to foster a sense of community. When you are given power by a community, you must act to better that community.

A major threat to communities is outside actors. One of the saddest moments in the history of masculinity was imperialism. Imperialism was presented as the manifestation of western masculinity. Men would go forth into the unknown in search of new lands to explore, expand, and exploit. In the age of discovery, those ideas were central to the concept of manhood.

The same language this book uses about the merits of space exploration would fit right in with a speech about exploring the Amazon Basin. The Western Empires talked about resource extraction the same way the International Monetary Fund would talk about development aid. Imperial dreams were cloaked in the language of charity and expanding civilization.

Western colonial and imperial powers, driven by greed, waged genocide on native populations by enslaving them or marginalizing them. In Australia, the colonial government established and ran boarding schools for Aboriginal children. They were taken from their parents and enrolled into disciplinarian schools that sought to force western assimilation. Children were abused at these schools and "some never even made it out alive" (Van Krieken 2004). This practice continued until the 1970s.

Often, smaller folk cultures and indigenous communities with their own unique cultures are targets of moralists and nationalists. The role of masculinity is to protect these cultures, not destroy them in the spirit of western chauvinism. An important lesson for modern men is to learn to coexist with different communities and cultures. We must always find ways to cooperate so a minor difference doesn't become a lightning rod for conflict.

Another threat to communities is neglect. A community, like any relationship, needs constant work to maintain itself. Lazy men won't do the work necessary to maintain a healthy community; they let the world around them fall into disrepair. Rural Japan has fallen victim to the silent rot. Allan Richarz of Bloomberg notes, "With fewer young people and a glut of elderly residents—among the longest-lived in the world—many rural towns appear to be locked into a demographic death spiral. If current trends continue, by 2040,

869 municipalities—nearly half of Japan's total—will be at risk of vanishing, according to the Japan Policy Council. As many as 80 percent of municipalities in some prefectures may disappear over the next 40 years, their populations having shrunk beyond the point of viability" (2021). This is the sad reality of rural life. Due to a lack of transportation and job opportunities, young people are leaving the rural towns for cities like Tokyo and Osaka.

Many people don't want to leave their homes. Tokyo is already one of the most densely populated spaces in the world; more accumulation will further pollute the air and stymie the people. The United States has also followed a similar, if tamer, trend. California and the East Coast are crowded, but they are where the job market is the hottest.

One would think community would be rebuilt in cities, but that is not the case for all neighborhoods. Decisions regarding which type of infrastructure a city should create has drastic implications for the strength of communities.

American highways were designed with the expressly stated goal of uniting the country. Alana Semeuls of the *Atlantic* points out that the "1956 Federal Highway Bill created the pathway for a 41,000 mile interstate highway system, states and cities jockeyed for the funding to build ever-more extensive networks of pavement that could carry Americans quickly between cities" (2015). The walkability of cities is important, especially for younger men who don't have a car or license.

This infrastructure plan was an investment in uniting the diverse communities of America together, but due to poor planning it had the opposite effect. Highways bisected poor communities, many of which were Black and Latino, because they were the cheapest sections of land to build on. A loud overpass further devalued property in the area and created an economic dead zone within urban centers with the poorest people paid the highest price.

These dead zones created by neglect have real consequences. The first story that comes to mind for most people when they hear about dangerously high levels of lead in drinking water is the story of Flint, Michigan, a town that suffered major drinking water contamination from leaded pipes.

Unfortunately, Flint isn't alone. Olga Khazan of the *Atlantic* writes "about 5.5 million Americans in communities around the nation got their water from systems that exceeded the Environmental Protection Agency's lead action level of 15 parts per billion." Lead contamination "permanently lower[s] IQ and lead to behavioral problems. Lead's damage to the body is difficult to reverse and can last a lifetime" (2019). Fetal miscarriages and maternal health are also under threat from contaminated drinking water.

Most estimates posit it would cost nearly thirty billion dollars to remove lead from water infrastructure. We have known for years lead poisoning is contributing to increased crime, mental health issues, and educational failures in poor communities, but due to neglect, we haven't resolved the issue.

Masculinity must be the bulwark against the destruction of these communities. Individuals dedicated to masculinity must stamp out corruption that harms the best interests of their community. They must protect against the outside forces who hope to break the community. Young men must ensure their communities don't fall into disrepair and to heal the decades of neglect that have befallen them.

The first step in creating a healthy community is engaging with people. Introversion and extroversion are irrelevant in this discussion. We are social beings. It's important we know the people in our community and they know us. We must talk to our neighbors. Maybe that's in your cul-de-sac or your apartment building. We need to take steps to meet the people in our community.

An important part of engaging with people is punctuality. Weak men are terminally late at best, flakers at worst. A man's word in a community must mean something. When you promise to arrive at a community event at a certain time, you must move heaven and earth to keep that promise.

You do so out of respect. If people give you their time for anything, you must honor that time with your own. Late arrivals are not only harmful for trust, but they also hurt productivity. No mentor would waste their time—time spent working—on training individuals who disrespect time. If you are late to every meeting, you are harming everyone else who must waste time on waiting for you when they could be working. A man must keep his word, especially if it is regarding punctuality.

Another step in engaging in your community is volunteering. Many young men lack enough positive role models in their lives. Without engagement from the community, learning its importance is much harder. You can make the difference by doing something as small as coaching a little league team or math tutoring. These small actions strengthen a community and tell young men they aren't alone. If they have a problem, you can become another adult or role model to help them. Men get lost on the path to excellence and volunteering is a crucial step for them to find their way back.

One powerful addition to a community is business. The lack of economic mobility in rural communities is a big part of their decay. Bringing jobs and opportunity to a community give it the chance to flourish. New tax revenue can fund better infrastructure and amenities. Successful men can set better examples to younger boys who feel like they have nothing in their futures. One of the most powerful places I have ever seen this was in a barbershop. It was a business first and foremost, but it provided incalculable wealth to the whole community. Men would gather and talk about sports, music, politics with such passion with the necessary amount of respect to keep the atmosphere inviting. Sons would come with their fathers and learn how to talk to their elders and how to heed their wisdom. Certain businesses can provide that social space and the masculine man must support them for the strength of the community.

Some businesses fail to create a community. A firm like Uber which contracts all of its drivers incurs no obligation to the well-being of any community. Even traditional firms stop caring about the health of the communities around them after growing to a largescale size. If you feel your job isn't providing you with that sense of camaraderie your parents and grandparents reminisce about, then consider joining a worker cooperative.

A worker cooperative is a firm where the ownership of the firm belongs to those who work within it. Major decisions are voted on democratically, and the hierarchy is relatively small. Worker cooperatives tend to produce happier workers and they even seem to be more resilient than traditional firms (Olsen, 2013). During a downturn, a company may lay off some workers to save money. Unfortunately, that means they won't have those workers on hand when business returns. Worker's cooperatives inculcate such a strong sense of community many workers will choose to take temporary pay cuts so they may keep their coworkers employed. This way, they can hit the ground running when the market improves. Nothing says strong community quite like a worker cooperative.

In the modern world where we find ourselves alienated without a sense of community, masculinity is more important than ever. The idea of the self-made man is a fantasy, and we need men to build strong communities that produce even stronger men. Against corruption, outside actors, and neglect, men must be diligent in their involvement in their communities. We want men to find mentors and one day become mentors to ensure we can build upon the knowledge and wisdom of previous generations and push society forward. It is impossible to be a masculine man without creating a community around you.

CHAPTER 3

CHARISMA 1: GOOD

In 1815, Louis XVIII sent the 5th Infantry Regiment to Grenoble on orders to apprehend the former French Emperor Napoleon Bonaparte. Napoleon had escaped exile and was making his way to reclaim the throne. When faced by an army of his own former soldiers he removed his jacket and yelled into the crowd, "If any of you are brave enough to shoot your emperor, here I stand!" The men quickly forgot their mission and pledged themselves to Napoleon once again. Napoleon won an army off sheer charisma.

It's important to recognize the disposition of a leader. Everyone has a capacity for leadership, but that must be cultivated like any other skill. A leader will lead regardless of the situation or their rank. Sometimes the intern, with a better understanding of human behavior, must step up to fill the vacuum. A leader will step up when a situation demands.

Just as we use discipline to measure productivity, we use charisma to determine the efficacy of leaders. Charisma is the quality that commands attention and devotion in others. It goes beyond just being liked; it entails earning trust.

As men we are expected to be confident and charismatic. According to economist Linda Babcock, one of the reasons why women make less money than men even in the same profession and position is because "men initiate salary negotiations four times as often as women do, and that when women do negotiate, they ask for 30 percent less money than men do" (Babcock 2009). The confidence in one's ability and the charisma to convey it will yield returns.

Charisma is complicated to develop because its expression is unique to each individual. Charisma creates an audience. People who trust you and your intentions will place their faith in you. It becomes your responsibility to meet or exceed their expectations. Charisma allows you to effectively communicate your feelings and dedication because often, people don't care about how much you know until they know how much you care. A well-developed charismatic personality will naturally exude confidence, ending the need to fake it.

Charisma has three parts: attention capture, persuasion, and motivation. They work together to improve your reach and efficacy. If you struggle with any part, it'll be more difficult to manifest a healthy charismatic personality. They need to be second nature, done without any explicit intent. Inauthenticity is the greatest poison to charisma. The moment people realize you don't care about your role or their cause they will disregard you.

Capturing attentions is a delicate affair. If you do it well, you can attract new members to your endeavor, or ensure people who already follow you don't get distracted. A person obsessed with the limelight has no pure intentions for their advocacy or quest. Sometimes they're just nonsense grifters with deep insecurities. Often, it is people who fear they will be forgotten who act out for attention.

Ideally one would use provocative or enticing imagery. In psychology this is called the "foot-in-the-door" phenomenon. This is a tactic commonly used by sales representatives. The idea is by getting some modicum of attention or intrigue, you can build a relationship with your audience and convince them further. This book began by openly stating women are better than men. It's a rambunctious claim that is intended to cause a visceral reaction given the subject matter. It was both a challenge and an excellent introduction to the crisis of masculinity and why men are falling behind in the modern world. There was never any deception or inauthenticity.

Another way you can command attention is through action. Actions speak louder than words. If a group of your friends want to make plans for the holidays and you enter the conversation with a thought-out itinerary, you have immediately earned their attention. You have gone beyond the scope of the conversation. Now if they want to either argue for or against it, they will still need you in the conversation. If there is a hesitancy to act, be bold in your actions. Some effort is better than no effort.

There is a lot of psychological analysis on the importance of action. Ninety percent of communication is nonverbal, meaning messages are relayed before you even utter your first words. Albert Mehrabian writes in his 1972 book *Nonverbal Communication*, "When there are inconsistencies between attitudes communicated verbally and posturally, the postural component should dominate in determining the total attitude that is inferred."

Action on its own is rarely sufficient, especially if there is a crisis. A study published in *Leadership Quarterly* found "there are at least two forms of charismatic leadership under crisis conditions—visionary and crisis-responsive." Think of the visionary as a leader who spends his time investing in the group and a crisis-responsive being a leader who emerges to take the reins when the group is under duress. The study posits "once the crisis condition has abated, the effects of crisis-responsive leadership deteriorate comparatively faster than other forms of charismatic leadership" (Hamstra 2014).

A visionary leader is very outcome-oriented, they think about what there is to gain in any venture and how to motivate others for shared success. Steve Jobs is the quintessential example of a visionary leader. He had a strong affirmative vision regarding the aesthetic and functionality of Apple products, and worked tirelessly to reach them. He also had a reputation of being demanding and hard to work under, and that lead to his firing from the company.

A crisis-responsive leader is there to ameliorate conditions. It is a leadership style that focuses on present survival rather than opportunities to grow. Often when a company is struggling to turn a profit, new management is brought in to restructure the firm and turn it around. Private equity is built on this concept and creates an industry for crisis response.

Both of these leadership methods are valid and sometimes the way to materialize one's charisma is by playing to the leadership qualities needed: visionary in good times and crisis-responsive during hard times.

The next facet of charisma every man should master is persuasion. We are social creatures, and we rely on each other for survival. It is important we can persuade individuals to be charitable to our causes and goals. The three modes of persuasion are logos, ethos, and pathos.

Logos is logical persuasion via empirical analysis. This is more effective against a more educated audience and sometimes by itself can suffice. If I wanted to convince my audience a universal basic income (UBI) is a good idea, then I could start spouting facts on how it lowers poverty, improves mental health, and lowers crime. A well-constructed meta-analysis would go a long way to persuade my audience.

Ethos is convincing someone from an ethical argument. This is more effective against individuals with a strict moral compass. You need to make the moral argument a certain idea or action is the best to achieve their axiomatic belief. If my axiomatic belief is it is moral to increase human well-being and happiness, then making the argument an UBI will significantly increase happiness across society will be more compelling because I find it the most moral policy.

Pathos is the emotional appeal. These arguments appeal to our emotions or even self-interest. This appeal works well against people who tend to be overly emotional. An emotional appeal for UBI would start with a story, something that puts a face on the issue. The story would star a single mother in Stockton who used her UBI to pay for night classes to finish her bachelor's degree. The degree opened the door to a new job in a neighborhood and lifted her and her four-year-old daughter out of poverty.

Stories materialize the abstract concepts found in academic journals and economic studies. Unfortunately, many people still fall victim to their emotions, so understanding pathos and using it responsibly is a burden for every leader.

While it may be beneficial to be emotionally invested in an outcome or cause, letting those emotions run rampant is a threat. We are emotional beings, but we must master emotions to avoid acting on them. We should be in control of them, not the other way around. A general tip for life: never act under extreme emotions. If you aren't thinking with a clear head, you won't solve the problem—you will create more. Before my first jiu-jitsu tournament, I had spent hours on the mat everyday drilling different positions and attacks, but when I bumped hands against my opponent, my fear and excitement prevented me from using everything I learned. It was a new experience and I humiliated myself in front of my coach.

This competition taught me there were avenues where my resolve and self-control would be tested, so I immediately enrolled in the next tournament with better knowledge of what I needed to do to keep calm. Luckily for me, fighting isn't a realm where I practice persuasion, but we can still extract a lesson. If we make fools of ourselves while emotional, we send the message we cannot handle the pressure. The burden we bear is beyond our capacity and we are better off stepping down. You will demoralize people when they realize they can't place their faith in you, thus any charisma you began cultivating wanes.

The final part of charisma is motivation. A truly charismatic man will not only prove his authenticity and compel agreement, but he will also uplift the capacity of all who follow him. Charisma is not about you, but the people around you. Everyone has their issues and insecurities, but a charismatic man will render them moot by inspiring people.

Compliments are particularly important, especially if they are genuine. Simply saying someone is "chill" or "cool" rings hollow. You can say that about anyone. A genuine compliment is unique to the recipient. If your best friend lost unhealthy body fat then mention it. Exclaim how it inspires you and it speaks to his worth. Chances are, he's unhappy with his journey so far. He might have to cut out his favorite foods, feel miserable, and not see direct progress for lengths of time. Simply acknowledging his effort reassures him his journey is valid and motivates him to continue.

Praise is vital according to a study by Sho Sugawara, who found "praise following motor training enhances consolidation of the learned sequence since the rate of offline improvement was significantly greater" relative to those who didn't receive praise as a part of positive reinforcement. Praise has the added effect of improving learning. A "human neuroimaging study demonstrated that praise activates reward-related areas of the brain, specifically the ventral striatum. Rewards are associated with increased dopaminergic activity in the midbrain and striatum, in which dopamine-dependent long-term potentiation (LTP) has an important role in memory consolidation" (Sugawara, 2012).

Building a good rapport with all the people in your life is important, but to do so you need to understand their struggles and their trauma. We are insecure beings. We constantly doubt ourselves and people are all too eager to point out our flaws. Acknowledging their strengths goes a great distance in them overcoming feelings of inadequacy. This doesn't mean you sing everyone's praises like a sycophant. If praise is cheap it loses value and suddenly feels disingenuous. Ideally, a compliment is timed for maximum effectiveness and includes constructive criticism.

Another way to motivate people around you is by setting a positive example. I mentioned earlier actions speak louder than words. This becomes doubly true when motivating someone. When you set a positive example by breaking a record, taking a proactive action, or creating an innovative solution to a problem, you implicitly broadcast the message everyone can succeed—they can do the same thing you're doing.

When you motivate someone, the intention is to uplift them beyond their current capacity. You need to understand the strengths and potential of anyone you're working with. You need to understand their demeanor and personality because everyone has a unique communication style that resonates with them. A peer-reviewed study by evolutionary anthropologist Roman Stengelin shed interesting insights on how praise can develop the brains of young children. He finds "experiencing positive emotions through collaboration may boost children's prosocial behaviors by motivating them to join and help in adults' activities, or to build positive reputations with potential collaborators" (Matsudaira, 2016).

Charisma carries a promise of success. A charismatic leader makes an unspoken promise his leadership is vindicated by his results. A charismatic leader understands the strengths of his friends, family, peers, and students. He plays to those strengths and creates systems that ensure win-win outcomes. Charisma removes hostility and insecurity from social spaces and creates the environment for real personal fulfillment.

I would like to offer my friend Benjamin Oswald (not a real name) as an example. He ran a non-profit while we were both in high school and had a lot of power in his organization. As head honcho it was his job to make sure everyone hit their targets. Him being a lot younger than his underlings made that challenging. When you challenge someone's ego, even unintentionally, your charisma sunders. A high school kid managing a non-profit staffed by college volunteers walks on thin ice and Benjamin, with all his competence, overstepped his boundaries frequently.

One time a volunteer who worked under him, a woman by the name of Janet (also not a real name) fell behind on creating an important calendar. Now, a non-profit must follow strict rules regarding their conduct lest they face an audit that delays their operations. When Janet fell behind in creating their fall calendar, it was up to Benjamin to hold her accountable. It was a tough situation because they were both on friendly terms, but Benjamin was quick to point out blame. After many passive aggressive emails, he finally called her and confronted her on the phone. She accused him of micro-managing, something he felt he needed to do with her failing to meet their deadline. He accused her of being unproductive and began yelling.

When he recounted the story to me, I asked him if he wanted to go for a walk and cool off. Benjamin was clearly overwhelmed by running an operation while dealing with the stresses of our admittedly competitive high school.

His goal as the president of a debate league was to ensure the organization ran smoothly. When he confronted Janet, he did so to lay blame and vent his frustrations. He failed his objective, and worse, ruined an amicable working relationship and genuine friendship.

One lesson I've learned, and try my best to use, is the positive image of others. Men are usually starved of compliments and that leaves many of them insecure. Creating a positive self-image forces people to live up to that and motivates them to fix their blunders without ever needing to be threatened. Instead of a carrot and stick approach, you convince the stubborn mule he is a glorious mustang. To prove himself, he will have no choice but to run or admit to himself he is a failure.

I asked Benjamin a vital question: "Do you care more about feeling good or doing good?" Dumbstruck, he asked, "What kind of question is that?" I told him sometimes ego gets in the way of effective solutions and while he was right, he might need to swallow his pride to get his colleague to cooperate. This was something I'd had to do in an argument a few weeks prior.

I offered him a strategy: to resolve the problem with humility. I told him to apologize to Janet in the most sincere and gratuitous way possible to fix their relationship first before addressing the elephant in the room. I told him to avoid placing blame and praise her instead. By admitting he was stressed by the deadline and unjustly took his anger out on her, he showed he was also in the wrong. He acknowledged she was a hard worker and great volunteer (though she hadn't been so far) and she was also struggling with the craziness of their season.

By affirming her struggle, he created a window and an expectation. People care a lot about their self-image. We have grandiose beliefs about ourselves and our capabilities. By inflating a person's self-image, you create a positive stress on them to try and live up to the ideal. Benjamin, by painting Janet as conscientious and diligent volunteer, created an incentive for her to live up to a positive image rather than focusing on avoiding a negative label.

This tactic worked wonders. After three days, she had completed the perfect itinerary for the organization, one far better than her previous showings. By showing compassion he not only motivated her to get her work done, but to go above and beyond her station. To keep her self-image intact, Janet felt the need to show outstanding work to make up for failing to meet deadlines.

If we were to do a post-mortem analysis of the situation, the reason why I played a pivotal role in addressing Benjamin's struggle was because I was an independent actor. I wasn't emotionally involved in the outcome, so I had a much cooler head than Benjamin who just hours prior to coming to me had bloodied himself in a verbal firefight. Benjamin was a highly intelligent guy, in many ways much more so than me, but he had blind spots. Leadership is complicated. I had previous experience as Benjamin's debate captain, but my true strength was humility. You cannot learn or grow when your ego sucks the oxygen out of the room. Benjamin's pride prevented him from sympathizing with Janet, thus snowballing the problem.

Unlike Benjamin, I had spent a lot of time pondering the nuances of charisma. The summer before our junior year, I read Dale Carnegie's classic *How to Win Friends and Influence People*. My uncle, who understood my past struggles, recommended the book to me and it provided great insight to the nature of influence. Carnegie explains succinctly "that most people waver between the rational and emotional" or logos and pathos (1964). When emotions run high and making an emotional appeal becomes a useful method of communication. By prostrating himself, Benjamin healed Janet's bruised pride and calmed her down. That created the space for a rational plan to solve their problem.

I have no doubt admitting fault was a tough pill for Benjamin to swallow. From his perspective, he's the hardworking boss with ungrateful employees. Sure, he may have lost his cool, but his anger was righteous. But if he had stuck to his guns, he would be an ineffectual leader because leadership isn't about you. It's about the people around you. As a leader you're accountable to their well-being and true charisma is created by aligning one's success with the success of those he works with.

In conclusion, people are messy. We have our grab bag of insecurities, idiosyncrasies, and destructive habits. A charismatic leader will always find himself weeding through the noise to find some semblance of success. It takes great mental and emotional fortitude to take up the mantle of a leader. Not everyone is strong enough to step forward when chaos strikes. An important place to start is by measuring your success with how successful you make others. That is the secret to the charisma of man.

CHAPTER 4

CHARISMA 2: EVIL

———

One can think of no greater force wielded by man than charisma. A person is charismatic when they can inspire devotion and command attention from others. Charisma will build civilizations and sunder empires. The previous chapter talked at length about how the reader must be more charismatic to express themselves.

Unfortunately, charisma has a dark side that will cause harm to you and people around you. This chapter wants to give you the tools to identify when charisma is evil.

People don't care about how much you know until they know how much you care. Your charisma will be earned when you prove to those around you your interests in their mutual cause are genuine and altruistic. The problem with ethos is it is easily bought.

Bill Gates is an interesting character. As one of the wealthiest men to ever live, he pledged to donate his wealth to the betterment of humanity. His ex-wife and him have done important work in addressing infant mortality and pushed for improving access to potable water in developing African countries. If that were all he did, he would be a hero for using his intellect and wealth to bring the world's foremost experts to address genuine problems afflicting the global south. I would argue we haven't seen the whole truth behind his endeavors and the few glimpses we have betray a much more dangerous state of affairs.

To understand Bill Gates, we need to understand the source of his charisma. Founded in 2000, the Bill and Melinda Gates Foundation is a philanthropic non-profit. They have partnered with the United Nations and the World Health Organization to distribute vaccines and medical supplies in Africa and even fund internet access in public libraries in the United States. "The foundation funds vaccinations through programs like GAVI, which Gates set up with a $750 million grant in 1999 and which is estimated to have saved millions of lives" (Piper 2020). He has shown a proven track record to do good, but reality is not a high-budget superhero movie; there are no perfect good guys who will solve the world's problems.

Recently, their foundation partnered with Oxford University and the drug maker AstraZeneca to develop a COVID-19 vaccine. Originally, Oxford University had plans to create the vaccine without a patent so the vaccine would be free for everyone around the world to use. Weeks after the announcement, Oxford reversed course and signed a deal with Astra-Zeneca to give them exclusive rights to produce the vaccine at the behest of the Gates Foundation. The Bill and Melinda Gates foundation provided crucial funding for research on the virus and thus had enormous power in pressuring Oxford.

When asked about lifting intellectual property protections and patents on mRNA technology, Gates replied, "Well, there's only so many vaccine factories in the world and people are very serious about the safety of vaccines. And so moving something that had never been done — moving a vaccine, say, from a [Johnson & Johnson] factory into a factory in India — it's novel — it's only because of our grants and expertise that that can happen at all" (Quelly 2021). This was proven false when the Associated Press found three major factories "whose owners say they could start producing hundreds of millions of COVID-19 vaccines on short notice if only they had the blueprints and technical know-how. But that knowledge belongs to the large pharmaceutical companies who have produced the first three vaccines authorized by countries including Britain, the European Union and the U.S. — Pfizer, Moderna and AstraZeneca. The factories are all still awaiting responses" (Cheng 2021).

Why did a man who made his money on personal computing come to become the single greatest private authority on vaccine distribution? It comes from his mastery of ethos. He doesn't need to have any personal expertise when he can hire any expert in any field. We trust that because he has the money to not spare a single expense, he will hire the greatest minds in the world—and to some extent this is true, but is an incomplete picture.

Private-public partnerships like the ones Gates sought with NGOs and governments require an immense investment in ethos. Lawmakers need to convince their constituents the plan is viable and stake their own reputation on the promised success of the partnership. Making descriptive statement like the efficacy of a vaccine is usually relegated to the experts, but the descriptive claim regarding the distribution of that vaccine is a question of incentives. Gates used his charisma to sell win-win-win plans and the expertise he courted played a pivotal role in that.

The problem with Bill Gates interfering in vaccine development is it muddies the water regarding his true intentions. If one were charitable, they could rationalize his strong arming of Oxford University as a play to liberalize vaccine development and increase production. There is some evidence for this as AstraZeneca has pledged to make the vaccine profit free for the duration of the pandemic.

Unfortunately, this policy, even if noble, is insufficient. Astra-Zeneca and other vaccine makers like Pfizer and Moderna could not produce vaccines fast enough even with help from western governments. The reflex to protect intellectual property meant a delay in vaccine distribution in the global south. That delay cost lives. And with hindsight being twenty-twenty, privileging the perspective of a billionaire over those of local actors in developing countries adds countless more to the tally of lives lost to charisma.

Bill Gates doesn't need to build his charisma with conspiracy theorists, they thankfully have very little power in the grand scheme of things. Instead, his influence is through spheres of power. Every year, academics, politicians, celebrities, and business moguls convene at the World Economic Forum in Davos where they discuss global trends. Gates has a lot of influence in this arena. He can always lobby governments for what he believes will result in positive change.

Experts and analysts are frequently proven wrong in hindsight, but we still defer to their judgment because we believe they are more likely to be right because of the hours they put into honing their craft. I would largely agree with operating this way. The magic of charisma is you don't need the ethos developed by an impressive resume when you can just borrow the expertise.

We heed the scientific consensus as the highest point of logos because every field publishes thousands of peer-reviewed papers to reach the greatest certainty humanly possible. A single expert is different because they may hold some views that go against scientific consensus. They may be right and vindicated in the future, but a layperson who cannot grapple with the nuance and complexity of their positions must rely on the consensus of the experts. The respect a single expert gains comes in the form of ethos, a trust in their resume.

When a person is afraid, they'll flock to the first person they believe will fix their problems. Bill Gates wasn't the only voice in the room, but he was the loudest and most compelling. Charisma is often a signaler of competence. We sometimes justifiably think because someone can speak with confident authority on a given subject, they have the knowledge and insight to back it up. Unfortunately, that leaves people vulnerable to salesmen, some of whom just want to sell snake oil.

Now, one could handwave away the dangers of charisma as people just listening to poor data. While not ideal, it wasn't evil. A reasonable person would agree with you deception isn't intentionally evil, but there is more to charisma than deception. Charisma compels evil.

Good soldiers follow orders, and that is a problem.

During the Nuremberg Tribunals, many Nazi officers and collaborators gave the same defense of their heinous actions by claiming they were just following orders. Nearly everyone who gave that defense was hung. It is disheartening to know so many people could have been this callous to human suffering. You might be thinking to yourself, "How could so many people do something so horrific?" Sadly, it will shock you to know what happened in Nazi concentration camps was not a unique phenomenon. It happened before the Nazis and it has happened countless times after.

Yale, 1963. Stanley Milgram has subjects walk into a test laboratory. They are told they will be making important contributions to the study of learning and memory. Milgram wanted to know if, under compulsion, he could convince educated college students to take a life on orders. The methodology of the study brought test subjects into a fake research experiment. Trained actors would play subjects strapped down to an uncomfortable chair and hooked up to an ominous machine. The research assistants would ask the actual subject to help administer a memory test to improve the understanding of human cognition and cure mental ailments.

The subjects were asked to administer electric shocks when the actor answered incorrectly to the series of questions or failed the task. The actors would cry out in pain and plead for the experiment to stop, but the "teachers" were instructed by the lab assistants to continue the experiment. The shocks ranged from fifteen volts, moderate, to 450 volts (labeled fatal), and the lab assistant would prompt the subject to increase the voltage. The prompts ranged from, "Please continue," to, "The experiment requires you to continue," to finally, "The results are essential for the greater good" (Mcleod 2017).

The actors responded to the increasing voltage by crying and begging. The subjects were hesitant but proceeded with the experiment. Nearly two-thirds of the participants delivered the lethal shock and all of them made it to at least three hundred volts. A major criticism of this experiment was it only included men and women were less likely to administer fatal shocks in follow up studies. This is a valid point, but the aim of this book is to understand masculinity and the behavior of men. According to this experiment nearly two-thirds of all men could be hung under the Nuremberg Laws.

Milgram's study was about obedience, but it gives us important insights into the nature of charisma. Milgram theorized individuals follow two paradigms in social situations: "the autonomous state – where one takes responsibility for their actions as an independent actor — and the agentic state – where one passes off the consequences to the one who gave them orders, acting as agents for someone else's will."

Charisma is dangerous because it allows a strong-willed and persuasive individual to overtake the agency of others. If a man isn't held personally responsible for his actions, he can cause great pain. We are taught from birth to obey authority, starting with our parents and teachers. Savvy media personalities, strongmen, and religious leaders utilize that inherent conditioning to control their audiences. The disrepair of agency traps people in abusive relationships and cults.

How do we control the negative aspects of charisma? We must stay vigilant. It is important to always be skeptical of people with great charisma and great power. This doesn't mean we subscribe to every conspiracy theory under the sun. It means we take time to understand how systems of power work and what the proposed changes or ideas do to those systems. The problem with anti-vaxxers is they don't understand anything about biology or modern medicine. Their skepticism and objection come from an emotional and ignorant place. Unlike a scientist who is trained in the art of scientific skepticism that uses statistical analysis and scientific theory to investigate claims, they don't care about a deeper understanding of the world.

These are emotional reactions to an unsafe and chaotic world. There is an impulse to trust confident and charismatic people who make their words dramatic but accessible. The truth about vaccines and medicine is complicated and boring. If it weren't, medicine would not be a respected and well-paying profession.

There is an important way to be skeptical. It begins at understanding intent, systems, consequences, and power. Often, conspiracy theorists ascribe evil intent to a group of people unjustly. Nazis, before they ever mentioned putting Jews on trains to Treblinka, muddied the water with conspiracies of a Jewish world order that undermined German sovereignty. But there existed no international cabal against the German people. They accused the Jews of hoarding all the wealth and creating the economic crisis in the Weimar Republic. But that was the result of a global depression and heavy war reparations from France.

This phenomenon is making a comeback. Political figures like Jordan Peterson weaponize reactionary rhetoric to sell their brand. Jordan Peterson has made a name for himself opposing the "woke" post-modern neo-Marxism that pervades academia. That rhetoric closely parallels the "Cultural Marxism" conspiracy theory posed by White-Nationalists and Neo-Nazis in the US. Bill Berkowitz writes for the Southern Poverty Law Center cultural Marxism is a "conspiratorial attempt to wreck American culture and morality [and] is the newest intellectual bugaboo on the radical right... The very term, 'cultural Marxism,' is clearly intended to conjure up xenophobic anxieties" (Berkowitz 2003).

His passionate followers consider Peterson as some sort of intellectual messiah, but his charismatic persona has been built on a grift. He might not be an anti-Semite, but the rhetoric he uses could irresponsibly cultivate those tendencies in his audience.

They don't realize the consequences of falling for these conspiracies has created a new dogmatic following around fascism. The creation of a crisis and an overarching plot to resolve the fictional crisis is the weapon-du-jour of dictators and strongmen. You cannot build a cult of personality without showcasing an intrinsic value. Most dictators come to power off the backs of an illustrious military career. Some of them take the added step of revising history to make themselves seem larger-than-life. A cult of personality is a useful tool to control people because when you indoctrinate them with a terrifying threat, you can sell yourself as the solution.

Charisma can do great harm because it binds people into groups. If those groups are founded on hate and lead by monsters, that charisma becomes a weapon of mass evil. This book concerns itself with the proliferation of positive masculinity. For a man to harness the benefits of charisma, he must be ready to accept challenges to his authority and work with dissenters. True charisma doesn't need deception or the creation of imaginary enemies. Charisma is about uplifting people, not crushing an enemy.

CHAPTER 5

RAISON D'ETRE

T.S. Eliot's *The Wasteland* tells the story of a society in decay. This story of man falling into pit of despair follows the parallel between the legend of King Arthur and the post-war trauma and disillusionment plaguing the western world in the 1920s. Eliot conveyed men were falling apart and the only way to escape the wasteland they'd built around themselves was by finding magical words of wisdom that would heal all wounds and help the wandering youth escape the wasteland. The words he finds are the Sanskrit words spoken by the Thunder, "Datta, Dayadhvam, Damyata." This roughly translates to give to others, to show them compassion, and learn self-control.

On its own it is great general advice, which is why Canadian psychologist Jordan Peterson follows similar sentiments. In his books *12 Rules for Life: An Antidote to Chaos* and *Beyond Order: 12 More Rules*, he is fascinated with the idea of controlling the chaos and find meaning by creating order in one's life. Unfortunately, Peterson takes this a step too far in his attitude regarding activism. In *12 Rules for Life*, he notes "the proper way to fix the world isn't to fix the world. There's no reason to assume that you're even up to the task. But you can fix yourself. You'll do no one any harm by doing so, and in that manner at least, you will make the world a better place" (Peterson, 2018).

English writer and poet T.S. Eliot believed only a well-adjusted and successful individual has the moral right to change the world. That thinking is incredibly myopic. Masculinity is about fixing problems, not ignoring them. While it is true people who educate themselves and are organized in their pursuits tend to be more effective at reaching their goals, they are not the only ones who are allowed to engage with the world.

Both Eliot and Peterson ignore the role activism has in creating better people. Finding a cause or purpose gives many young men the spike of energy to engage in their community. To engage in any endeavor, you must have the courage to try even in the face of failure. If you care about your cause, you'll develop the right attitude very quickly and start learning from your missteps.

If you listen to Peterson's advice and let the fear of failing chill your efforts, your ability to grow is no longer bolstered by a selfless desire. Waiting to get the approval of entrenched systems before changing them is not always feasible, especially if the system itself is the problem. We make ourselves better by trying to make the world better.

We have a limited time on this planet, and it is our prerogative to decide what we do with it. There is a deep insecurity in all people regarding their worth. Did they use their time properly? Will they be remembered for their work, or will they die as a nobody?

Men need a cause to drive their lives because it forms an important part of their identity and it challenges them to be better. They need to strive for an ambitious goal far greater than themselves. It should play to their strengths and build on top of them. A cause should not get resolved in a few months of tepid work. Such a cause requires no sacrifice or growth. The cause should answer deeper questions about your purpose and should stimulate you intellectually, socially, and spiritually.

Your cause should demand a lifestyle change from you. You live your best life when you are challenged by the weight of your undertaking. The cause must force you to better yourself each day and motivate you to be your best self. This cause should also ensure it helps you form positive social connections. We are all influenced by the people around us. As such, it is imperative we surround ourselves with people who understand our drive. Your cause should be a tool to create healthy social relationships.

There are two types of causes. I like to call them Type A causes and Type B causes. Likewise, there are two types of great men: those who push humanity forward and break the barriers previously thought impenetrable and those who ensure as humanity marches forward, no one is left behind. It is exceedingly rare a person is entirely in either camp. Most endeavors have a synergy of Type A and Type B energy.

The Type A cause concerns itself with exploration and pioneering a new idea. This characteristic attracts people like scientists and artists who concern themselves with pushing boundaries. A person with a proclivity for Type A causes is obsessed with intense research and the experience of new ideas. They are so dissatisfied with the status quo they do whatever they can to change it. Their enthusiasm is easily mistaken for hyperactivity and occasionally diagnosed as ADHD or ADD by overzealous counselors. A study by Dr. Megan Fresson at Université de Liège, Liege, Belgium found "the stereotype describing boys as inattentive and impulsive might contribute to the overdiagnosis." In a prescriptive study they found that therapists internalized negative stereotypes "of boys as inattentive and impulsive, leading stigmatized boys to mimic the pattern of results that a child with ADHD [would display]" (Fresson, 2019). Boys are far more likely to receive an ADHD diagnoses and internalize that as a character flaw. It is not a flaw. If channeled responsibly, it could help young men achieve great things.

You may be forgiven for thinking the most important attribute to pursue a Type A cause is intelligence, but you couldn't be further from the truth. Intelligence is great, but it isn't rare. Anyone with sufficient dedication can become competent at any task. Talent may give some people a greater return on investment for time spent learning a new skill, but isn't necessary to be Type A-driven. The most important characteristic is courage—courage to fail.

One victory is built on a mountain of losses. People rarely succeed on their first shot, and some people never succeed even after their one-millionth shot. To win, one must be comfortable with losing. You need to have a certain humility and courage to admit when you are wrong or when you have failed and immediately have the energy to bounce back and try again.

If you respond with a smile to the knowledge you only have a 0.6 percent chance of succeeding at a task, there is a good chance you will be attracted to a Type A cause. Inhibitions, fear of failure, embarrassment—those mean nothing to you. Your will should stay strong and never get derailed by social pressure. Often, you must prepare to stand strong, even if you stand alone.

To pursue a Type A cause, one must be prepared to build on top of the work of others. No man triumphs alone and, usually, they have a team or a mentor whose ideas influence and augment one's own. To reach new heights, you must be wise enough to stand on the shoulders of a giant. One cannot afford to grow arrogant or be deluded by their success. A Type A cause requires constant and humble dedication to the truth, and one cannot afford distractions.

Nikola Tesla is a prime candidate for the quintessential Type A-driven man. He dedicated his faculties from a young age to the pursuit of knowledge. After flunking out of college and gambling away his tuition money, Tesla found himself on a ship to the United States in 1884 with four cents in his pocket. He began his work under Thomas Edison and was pivotal in the development of the DC (direct current) motor. "He was able to develop a successful system, but for business reasons, Edison decided not to use it." Naturally, Tesla was disappointed and also miffed because Edison did not offer him a bonus for completing the system. Tesla quit "in disgust. He then patented his system independently and entered into a business arrangement with another company to market it" (Rutgers, 2013).

Tesla's biggest failure after coming to America was his poor understanding of social systems. Many would grow heartbroken over losing such an idea to a shrewd businessman like Edison, but Tesla didn't let his dreams die at General Electric. Finding a job as a ditch digger that paid only two dollars per day, Tesla spent two years working on his next invention.

After partnering with George Westinghouse, Tesla began creating the infrastructure for the Alternating Current. AC had many advantages over DC. It was cheaper, could travel longer ranges, and used thinner wires. It would have been a slam dunk had Edison, the current owner of DC patents, not launched a smear campaign against AC. During this "War of the Currents," Edison "spread misinformation saying that alternating current was more dangerous, even going so far as to publicly electrocute stray animals using alternating current to prove his point" (Lantero 2013).

Tesla, needing to win back his reputation and pride, did the unthinkable. He offered himself as a conductor of AC current. During the 1893 World's Columbian Exposition, Tesla used AC transformers to light two lightbulbs held in his hand. Instead of wiring the lightbulb to the generator, he used his body as a wire to conduct the electricity through his arms. When the lightbulb lit, everyone was convinced AC was safe. The war was won.

Unfortunately, Tesla's story doesn't end there. After relinquishing his patents to Westinghouse—a move that lost him an untold amount of money—Tesla struck out independently. His failures went on. In 1895, a fire burned down his laboratory and destroyed his notes and prototypes. He had to restart from scratch. In 1898, his demonstration of a wirelessly controlled boat was widely denounced as a hoax, causing him to lose credibility in the media. In 1905, his project for creating a wireless radio transceiver capable of sending radio signals across the Atlantic went over budget. The chaos led his chief backer, one J.P. Morgan, to pull funding (Encyclopædia Britannica, 2021). The loss of J.P. Morgan was his greatest defeat. His multitude of ideas was constrained to the depths of his notebooks without adequate funding. Tesla's reputation was so thoroughly dragged through the mud he could never again find an investor to back his revolutionary but eccentric projects.

He died without ever winning the Nobel Prize, as was his dream ever since he'd convinced his father to let him pursue engineering. But after his death, the scientists who built on his innovations vindicated him. He was a Type A because the only thing that stopped his desire for discovery was his own death. Even after his passing, his research opened doors to new possibilities of research.

There are a few criticisms leveled against people who are too radical or too free-thinking. The most ubiquitous one is they usually turn out wrong. That isn't a criticism. The path to being right involves discarding a lot of wrong ideas. It is true wrong ideas can hurt people. For the longest time, doctors used to believe in bloodletting, but doing nothing seals error in perpetuity. When one is on the frontier of knowledge, mistakes will be made.

Another criticism is many pet projects, while interesting, are not direly needed. Why go to Mars when we struggle to feed people here on Earth? I sympathize with such sentiments because it is infuriating to see resources wasted on fruitless endeavors, but we must remain cognizant of the nature of discovery. The space race, for example, was a scientific boon for ordinary citizens. Even though only a handful of people visited space, space travel was the essential building block of satellite communication and GPS. Experiments in zero gravity have yielded new discoveries in biology and material sciences. ZBLAN, "a fiber optic material that may lead to much lower signal losses per length of fiber than anything that can be made on Earth," can revolutionize data transmission. "It is currently under testing onboard the International Space Station" (Greenblatt, 2019). Just because a technology or discovery is not immediately useful doesn't mean future generations can't derive value from it. Any activity that pushes humanity's understanding of the universe forward is a gift to everyone.

The biggest criticism I hear—one which I think is the most relevant—is pioneers alienate people who can't keep up with their pace. This is undoubtedly an issue. Tesla, as brilliant as he was, chased away his investors through his eccentric demonstrations. His lack of business acumen led him to squander the usefulness of so many of his inventions. The answer is taking the influence of Type B thinking and incorporating it in the delivery of your idea.

The Type B drive concerns itself with the question of people and power. How does one's ambition affect the people around oneself? A Type B cause tries to answer that question through its machinations. Common Type B drive people include social workers, teachers, businessmen, and politicians. They derive their power and legitimacy by how they directly touch the lives of people. It was a team of engineers who built the iPhone, but it was Steve Jobs who made it a success. Columbus showed

America to the European powers, but it was Ferdinand and Isabella who organized the conquest of the new world.

The Type B cause takes the contributions of Type A and devises a plan to wield them in the service of people or power. Instead of courage, the most important attribute for the success of Type B causes is patience. Those who dedicate all their resources to winning the battle will fall to those who dedicate themselves to winning the war. Strategy is incredibly important for success, whether that involves convincing your child to eat their vegetables or leading an army. The impatient will hastily make mistakes, something you cannot afford if you are Type B. While Type A is encouraged to make mistakes, Type B cannot be so flippant. When wielding a sword, mistakes are deadly.

The Type B-driven man finds himself in complicated systems where uncertainty reigns supreme. Small differences in a system of great power can have enormous consequences. A Type B-driven man will take that statement to heart. To do good, there will be very few celebrations or admiration. Type B concerns itself far more with doing good than with being right.

My favorite example of a Type B-driven person is Bernie Sanders. From his 2020 campaign slogan, "Not me. Us," to his decision to host an LGBT pride parade as Mayor of Burlington, Vermont in 1983, he has demonstrated a drive to wield power for the good of ordinary people. His contributions are difficult to unpack because he often stands alone.

In an interview in 2005 for journalist Matt Taibbi of the *Rolling Stone*, then-congressman Bernie Sanders recounts how he got the nickname The Amendment King. "Nobody knows how this place is run," says Rep. Bernie Sanders. "If they did, they'd go nuts" (2020). He was an independent, a self-described socialist under the Bush years. In one year, he would be the first independent elected as a senator.

Sanders guided Taibbi through the cavernous legislative process. He passionately believed "people need to know" when the systems of government fail to function. To pass an amendment onto an existing bill, you need to get passed the House Rules Committee who has the power to kill any amendment on the spot. The chairman is handpicked by the Speaker of the House and is rewarded for party loyalty. Unfortunately, it's not the only committee that stands in the way of legislation. The Judiciary committee can kill a bill if the chairman "got up mid-meeting and killed the lights, turned off the microphones and shut down the C-SPAN feed" (Taibbi, 2005). Such tactics are common if you wish to ensure nothing gets done.

In such a sluggish environment, how did Bernie Sanders pass more roll-call amendments (those that get a vote on the House floor) than any other member of the House of Representatives? Sanders' investment in his independent status is the secret to his success. Rather than playing in simple left-right teams, he invested his resources in finding common ground. He worked with Republican Jeff Flake to end warrantless searches of bookstores and libraries and sunset provisions for the Patriot Act. It may sound modest, but some positive change is always better than no change.

Senator Sanders' drive to represent his community and working people at large stem from his early love of sports:

"Sanders had just turned 16 and friends say he was devastated after Dodgers owner Walter O'Malley announced the transfer" (Carpenter, 2015). The Brooklyn Dodgers had been grumbling about moving to Los Angles for years, but once they secured the funding, they jumped ship. "The Dodgers had been an essential part of his childhood in the Flatbush section of Brooklyn where he could walk to their ballpark, Ebbets Field, and buy a ticket for 60 cents." That event from his halcyon days shaped his understanding of the relationship between business and community. As mayor of Burlington, he wanted to invest in local pride. He "also believed Burlington needed a baseball team like the Brooklyn of his childhood." He entered talks with the Eastern League franchise for a communally owned team where citizens could buy in as owners and root the team to the City. Sources conflict over why exactly the deal fell through, but then-Mayor Sanders was a hair away from building what he viewed as an important facet of his community.

In 2015, Hillary Clinton accused Bernie Sanders of getting nothing done while in the Senate. That would be a damning rebuke of the senator had it been true. In 2010, an article pointed out "Sanders has slipped funding for community health centers in several health care bills over the years… [that] secured $11 billion in funding for these federally subsidized clinics that, by law, must operate in communities considered medically underserved due to poverty" (Ludwig 2020). This one amendment increased the number of people receiving low-cost medical treatment from eighteen million to nearly twenty-six million. He's no fan of Obamacare, but through pragmatic legislation, he made a material difference in the lives of millions.

Bernie Sanders has a very coherent and compelling political philosophy centered around uplifting people from poverty and giving them what he considers necessities in a modern world. He is often accused of being radical, but he may be one of the most pragmatic legislators in the US. You may disagree with his ideas, which is your prerogative, but you cannot deny his drive to do good. As of September of 2021, Senator Sanders will be an octogenarian with a lifetime of accomplishments to look back on.

It is important not to look down on those with a Type B drive. While something like a vaccine is incredibly important, it is useless if it never finds itself in the hands of ordinary people. The Type B drive pushes people to make systems that uplift others. Without proper implementation, no discovery will ever reach its full potential. Without negotiation, discussion, or compromise, we would never get anything done. None of us is greater than all of us. Those who work on their Type B skills understand the value of any idea is best determined by its accessibility.

Neither Type A nor Type B reign superior over the other. Any meaningful endeavor will need both. You may be a research doctor at Moderna, researching the vaccine for COVID-19, but you will have to work in a group. In the group, there will be differences of opinion and arguments over the truth. The scientists can't split up and work on their own research because they cannot afford to waste time chasing dead ends. There is a responsibility for every member to be respectful and work together. There needs to be proper communication and cooperation for the endeavor to be successful. If you're only Type A, then you are going to be a liability. If you're only

Type B, you are deadweight. You cannot escape the fact you need to cultivate both sides of your personality.

This book is a hybrid of both, too. I analyze data from different cultures, time periods, and thinkers to create a new understanding of masculinity—the Type A component. However, the larger part of the book, centered around helping young men develop better masculinity, is an act of social service—the Type B component. To adequately write this book, I needed to understand the ways to strengthen both components. For you, my reader, I needed to dissect both parts and explain the strengths and sacrifice needed to cultivate each and the tools to combine them in a coherent and compelling cause.

This brings us to an important question. What is your cause? That question is not an easy one to answer because it is exceedingly difficult for most young people to identify their strengths. The better place to start is by identifying your interests. It is natural we get better at things we like because we spend more time honing the skills associated with that activity. Within your interests, begin searching for activities you can experiment with. There are two things everyone must try: creating and volunteering. These two actions begin answering the question of which Type of cause drives you. Type A-driven men want to spend their time creating something new or discovering something new. Things often interest them more than people. The Type B-driven man will find more interest in dealing with people than with things. If that is you, you will be drawn to places where you either work with people or compete against them.

Sometimes neither cause will be lucrative enough to build a life. Even if your cause is as small as a hobby, it will still drive you to be a more fulfilled version of yourself. Lucky are those whose cause financially supports them. Maybe one day your cause can financially support you too. If your dream is to direct a movie, then you can write your script, take lessons in your free time, and eventually save up to make an indie film if Hollywood doesn't green light you. Even if you fail, you have a story to tell.

It is important to be fair to yourself when judging your success. Does your cause provide value and happiness in your life? If the answer is yes, then it is already intrinsically successful. Does your cause help others? If the answer is yes, then it provides extrinsic success. A tremendously successful cause is one that has both intrinsic and extrinsic rewards. Those who work only for themselves end up burnt-out and resentful. Those who only work for others end up burnt-out and unhappy as well. You need the stability of both for your cause to elevate you.

CHAPTER 6

DISCIPLINE 1: FREEDOM

You will shoot yourself in the foot, I can guarantee that. Victory will be within your grasp, your dreams will come to fruition, only for you to lose focus once and lose everything. That is what it means to be a man.

Masculinity is coming to terms with your failure and finding the resolve to get back up. One of the most iconic quotes from the film *Rocky* is the line, "It ain't about how hard you hit. It's about how hard you can get hit and keep moving forward" (Stallone 2006). You will always face rejection, but that is not something you should ever worry about. Getting rejected hurts, but it means you are trying to do something greater than people's expectations. It means you are shooting for higher places. It is admirable to try even with the looming dread of failure; it means you haven't given up on yourself and there is still hope for you be become a greater man.

Unfortunately, people handicap themselves. As discussed in previous chapters, young men are more vulnerable to bad influences and complacent behavior. If a man is motivated to pursue a cause and better himself through it, he must arm himself with a plan and the discipline to stick to it.

According to retired Navy SEAL, Jocko Willink, "discipline equals freedom." As men we are constantly under bombardment from our vices, from our laziness, and from temptations. We can choose either to feed into them, or to rise above them. It is dangerous to live a comfortable life. The world will seldom warn you before a catastrophe strikes and the inability to cope with being outside one's comfort zone will doom a young man.

A lot of suffering is caused by a lack of structure in one's life. Suffering is when you cannot escape predictable pain. If you repeatedly stub your toe at the bottom of a stairwell you are suffering a malaise. It is an easy fix, but you still grow careless and find yourself in pain. We all know that procrastination increases our stress, but that rarely stops someone from waiting until the last minute. This carelessness creates suffering for many men and we need structure to combat our lack of discipline.

I want to challenge our understanding of willpower. There is no magical on or off switch that dictates if a man is willful and disciplined or not. It is a psychological phenomenon and everything psychological is simultaneously biological. Our willpower functions like a muscle. It can be trained and strengthened, but it can also weaken and atrophy. Just like any muscle, it can get fatigued as well. According to a paper published by the Association for Psychological Science, "Across four studies, our demand manipulation (high vs. low) was highly depleting because it robustly elicited strong effort and fatigue sensations" (Mischel 2011). That means while we can exert our will, whether it be for pain tolerance or resisting sweets, there is a threshold where we cannot control ourselves anymore.

The best place to start small is with sleep. My grandfather had a saying: "A man who cannot control his desire for sleep or food will never amount to anything in life." He was more correct than he realized on both of those points. Both sleep and diet play an important part in how our brains function and exert control over our bodies.

A study in *Sleep Medicine Review* found "children aged 6–8 and 9–12 years, respectively, showed that effects of sleep on the consolidation of hippocampus-dependent declarative memories are comparable to those in adults... sleep in children like in adults strengthens declarative memories" (Diekelmann 2011). Sleep is incredibly important because it improves our brain function and our bodily function and health.

A good example is memory. Whenever we learn something throughout the day, the information is stuck in our head. As we sleep, we encrypt that information and enforce it into our brain so we can recall it readily in the future. If you want to improve your grades, sleep will need to go hand in hand with responsible study habits for maximum retention of information. Many students pull stressful all-nighters before exams and ultimately sabotage their own success.

A study in the *Journal of Adolescence* had "findings extend previous knowledge by showing that the relationship of sleep duration with positive attitude toward life and school grades was partly mediated by daytime tiredness and behavioral persistence" (Perkinson-Gloor 2013). Adjustments of as small as twenty minutes showed significant gains in the educational achievement of adolescent boys. If we get proper sleep, our ability to remember information becomes so much stronger. And in fact, our ability to recall and be productive with that information improves as well. Sleep is incredibly important as a building block for us to start thinking about ourselves and ways we can reorient ourselves.

Food was the second part of my grandfather's equation and there is a lot of research as to why. A study from the *Personality and Social Psychology Review* found "acts of self-control deplete relatively large amounts of glucose. Self-control failures are more likely when glucose is low or cannot be mobilized effectively to the brain. Restoring glucose to a sufficient level typically improves self-control" (Gailliot 2007). A healthy diet is necessary to maintain regulated blood glucose levels. We need to treat food as fuel support, making sure our food is healthy and nutritious with all our macro and micro-nutrients.

A healthy diet has important ramifications for the creation willpower. Ego depletion is a threat to discipline because relying on inconsistent motivation rarely leads to success. It's the same reason why many people fail to keep up with their New Year's resolution—they treat positive changes as a novelty rather than a reality. Researchers found people who "exhibited ego depletion [made] more mistakes after the depleting task than after the nondepleting task" (Job 2010). This means general performance is also compromised when one's willpower diminishes.

While my grandfather was forward thinking about certain aspects of discipline, one he neglected was his physical fitness. Modern life is characterized by more sedentary work and leisure which means many of us are not getting the exercise our ancestors got.

Exercise is incredibly important for the brain and the body. It activates the brain by giving us new stimulus, and new athletic potential exercise improves our reaction time and increases our ability to stay focused on a task. It also increases our metabolism so we can enjoy more of our foods. It has huge benefits to our body: increasing our testosterone, our muscle mass, our bone density, our mobility, our joint flexibility, and overall improving our mood. Exercise doesn't drain you. You should never think of it that way.

A study on school children in Thailand found children who "did not manage their time well enough to allow for physical activity" cascaded into rising childhood obesity. Fortunately "after 8 months [of weight management seminars], results showed that high caloric dietary intake significantly decreased, aerobic exercise activity increased ($P < .001$) and prevalence of obesity declined from 19.3% to 16.8%" (Sirikulchayanonta 2011). Ask not for a lighter burden, but for a stronger back. Exercise is a great way to get a stronger back and to give you more energy—energy to take on more obstacles in your day.

The final step is time. Your time is valuable, so don't waste it. It's crucial we make plans about what we wish to accomplish in any given day, through any given week or month. Time is one of the most important resources humans have. In economics, the term opportunity cost is the time cost of any action. If you could make $120 by working an extra six hour shift, each hour of your life is worth twenty dollars. If you spend an hour a week scrolling through social media, you have spent twenty dollars to do so because that is what you have given up to enjoy Instagram.

The final thing we need to understand is while it's important to be disciplined, it's also important we learn how to enjoy our leisure. We are human beings, we are not perfect machines, we have our flaws, we have our weaknesses, and we also need our downtime to recover from them. We need places to center and find ourselves.

This doesn't mean you spend all of your time on Netflix or video games. But it means if you have done the hard work of discipline, you get to enjoy your freedom. Discipline equals freedom. It also means you have the freedom to do new things. If you keep in mind the opportunity cost of leisure, you owe it to yourself to enjoy your freedom. You gave up time and that means money. You should invest in your enjoyment.

If the most enjoyable activity in your life is playing a video game, make sure you enjoy it to the fullest extent. If it is not your greatest joy, then look elsewhere. Your leisure is just as valuable as your work and if you work hard, you must play hard.

Discipline doesn't appear overnight. It needs to be built slowly. Sometimes you'll find yourself drifting away from schedule and fading in and out. For example, if you're trying your best to get proper sleep, the first night you do a decent job, and the night afterward you do a better job. But the third night, because of stress, you can't sleep as well. The fourth night, not as bad but not as good. You'll find yourself falling into patterns; you need to start working with those and building on top of them. Because consistency is key here. Just one night of proper sleep doesn't change your life. But making sure you get the adequate amount of sleep as often as possible will make a huge benefit for you. And this needs to be built slowly. All the small differences over time can add up to a lot of change.

Doing something as simple as going for a run in the morning will drastically improve our mood, our cardiovascular health, and our mental health. And just doing it a couple of times even small and consistently gives us the room to start building. If you dedicate yourself to spending five minutes every day jump roping, then that five minutes can very easily be augmented to six, seven, eight. Then you decide, "Okay, I'm already jumping rope. Why don't I do a couple of push-ups, a couple of pull-ups, a couple of sit-ups, squats?" You start adding on to whatever base you already have whatever schedule you already have, much like Legos or building blocks. You're taking these modular parts of you and putting them together. They're held together by habit.

That is discipline: a structure to live a healthy life. Everyone must create a model where discipline doesn't eat your willpower, but helps you generate it. It's important all of these steps are taken slowly but consistently because the journey of a thousand miles begins with that one first step.

CHAPTER 7

DISCIPLINE 2: MASTERY

---

*"Women, children, and dogs are loved
unconditionally. A man is loved on the
condition he provides something."*

—CHRIS ROCK

One of the greatest hindrances to masculinity is patriarchy. Patriarchy is not just men ruling the world or having all the power. Patriarchy is the system where a man must prove his worth through power. On some level, that sounds amazing. As a society, we want men to compete against each other to make the world better. Unfortunately, a patriarchal system binds one's humanity to their productivity. Masculinity is greater than the digits at the end of your pay stub and the model of your car.

The purest expression of masculinity has and should forever remain one's mastery. Mastery is the art of building skill and competence in a specific field. Mastery is innately masculine because it allows men to prove their worth on a level playing field. The pampered heir to a royal bloodline has little value on a soccer field if he can't work with his team and score. The kid growing up in the favellas or banlieues who dedicated every waking moment to his craft can kiss his trophy and celebrate his triumph. If masculinity is driven by output and competition, mastery is one of the most integral components to its realization.

Practice makes perfect—a statement as beautiful as it is overly simple. Perfection does not exist and even if it did, it would be unattainable by creatures as crude as humans. The adage conveys the very true sentiment the investment into mastery will put us on the path to perfection. We are not meant to reach that destination, but rather to find meaning in the process.

The history of physics is the perfect introductory course to mastery. Until the nineteenth century, all physicists studied Newtonian physics. By that point, Isaac Newton's predictions held true and physicists could pat themselves on the back, proclaiming humanity had complete understanding of physics save for two issues—the first being the question of light and the second being the nature of subatomic particles in relation to light.

Solving the first proved to be a massive headache for scientists. They could not confidently state the nature of light and every time they tried, they got conflicting results. Thanks to the double-slit experiment, scientists were confounded over whether light was a particle or a wave. A wave disperses from its source and a particle moves in a concentrated direction.

When directed through double slits, light would pass through like a particle, but disperse on the other side like a wave. Eventually, the German physicist, Werner Heisenberg, concluded the answer would forever remain unknowable. Per his uncertainty principle, it will always be impossible to create a means for measuring the nature of light without obscuring the results (Collins 2009). In plain English, there are certain phenomena in the universe that have their nature changed by the very act of measuring them.

The idea physics was relative deeply disturbed scientists. All scientific pedagogy centered around the idea the natural world had order, there was an objective reality, and humans could one day comprehend the entirety of reality.

One of the promises of the rationalist movement was all questions could be answered by science, humanity could reach a mastery of the natural science. Scientists hoped mastery would elucidate many of the bigger questions about the universe including the purpose of humanity and the possibility of a creator. But some began to doubt the validity of the scientific process and human ingenuity itself. The greatest minds did not waver in their conviction to the truth.

Albert Einstein was one such mind. His theory of general relativity was a major step in unraveling the twisted net that would soon become the field of quantum mechanics. Most of what we know about electricity and magnetism came from discoveries made in this field. Many of Einstein's ideas would be proven wrong by his students and all those who came after him, but that is the nature of discovery.

Mastery requires a self-critical lens for growth. It's only natural to be enamored by one's own success—bragging rights are human rights after all. However, that isn't an excuse to stay complacent. Einstein's models were good enough to eventually help get us to the moon, but we need to put more effort if we ever want to explore the stars.

Science is the enterprise of replacing error with ignorance. Every question we answer generates ten more. Mastery in physics and all other scientific fields is not about a perfect explanation, but a better, more valid one.

Mastery is the salvation of the masculine man. A man must wake up every day with a purpose, a means of investing in himself to push himself and all those who depend on him forward. We need constant challenge in our lives. Much like muscular atrophy due to a lack of exercise, our minds and spirits decay if we are not sufficiently tested. One of the saddest states for a man is a lack of motivation. That state can quickly spiral into depression if left unchecked. We all need a process to build our skillset and one of my greatest examples is my jiu-jitsu instructor, Edmaicon Moraes.

Edmaicon, or Maicon as we call him, is a black belt in Brazilian jiu-jitsu. Getting a black belt is a herculean effort. It takes years of training, competition, and even teaching to get the rank. In the jiu-jitsu community, we joke we address black belts as "professor" because getting a black belt is the equivalent in getting a PhD. He has an inspiring story and mindset.

To get a sense of his personality I asked him to describe himself in two sentences. He answered, "I never give up. I can do anything as long as I believe in myself." He is an amazingly disciplined person. He started practicing at the age of fourteen. To him, jiu-jitsu "keeps him out of his comfort zone," and he adamantly believes "we should never become comfortable with life."

Maicon found his sport of choice because he "didn't need a team of twelve players like with football (soccer) and to practice against a team of another twelve players." He reminisced "growing up poor in Brazil was tough. You only had two options to get out of poverty if you were bad at school. Either you played a sport like football, or you started dealing drugs." I asked him if jiu-jitsu helped him escape that fate to which he replied, "Yes. [It] kept me focused and prevented me from falling victim to the bad influences around me."

Maicon spends hours on the mat each day drilling, sparring, and perfecting his technique. I asked him if he ever felt like quitting. "I cannot give up!" he all but yelled. "Jiu-jitsu is hard, but it taught me discipline. I have too much faith in myself to let setbacks stop me now. Jiu-jitsu gave me opportunities to support my family and come to America and compete for a world championship." For Maicon, jiu-jitsu is not just a sport, it is the lifeline holding his life together.

One of the struggles with success is the ensuing ego, something I had to ask Maicon about. How did he manage to stay extraordinarily humble despite winning a world championship? His take: "You must be humble. From white belt to purple belt, I had a big ego because I never lost. That was a huge mistake because I stopped growing. When I became a purple belt, I started losing because I closed my mind to any advice or knowledge others gave me. I had to learn the hard way to humble myself." I asked if he still felt that way sometimes, to which he responded, "Yes, ego is a part of you, but discipline applies to both your schedule and your mindset. I always have to catch myself from becoming arrogant."

Maicon teaches many children and young men, so I was curious what he thought about dealing with insecure children. He answered, "Many children are coming to class without confidence, they are shy, bullied in school, or have a lot of problems making friends." He alludes to a real fear many young people lack confidence in themselves because they don't feel like they have any value to offer the world. For him, mastery is a way to counter that self-doubt because it gives children an avenue to improve themselves, even if they are the only ones who see it.

The final two questions I asked gave me a better insight on mastery and masculinity: how do you balance being competitive with the pure form of the art and how do you feel about the fact you will never master jiu-jitsu? To the first, he thought for a minute before answering, "Competition is important for growth, but jiu-jitsu is more than competition. We spend a lot of time training for competition because we have a lot of professionals in the gym, and it is my focus when I fight in MMA. However, I understand that a lot of older people train in the gym and they just want to be healthy while a lot of women train for self-defense. We need to strike a balance between competition and the art. When we compete, we should stay focused, but we should always enjoy the process. After competition we should keep experimenting so we can grow. We need to be intense and playful to progress in jiu-jitsu." His response to the latter question was much shorter: "That's exactly why I love jiu-jitsu, there will always be something new. If a person says they know all jiu-jitsu, they tell the whole world they know nothing."

Maicon is the perfect spokesperson for mastery. His dedication to a craft helped him escape poverty and provide for his family. It opened avenues for him to grow and pass those nuggets of wisdom onto others. At the age of twenty-six, he has more humility and wisdom than students twice his age. Mastery provides a man with a sense of worth and the motivation to seize the day. His dedication to the sport opened doors that would have stayed closed in the favellas of Brazil. Others may waste their time or spend it hedonistically, but Maicon chose to spend it on himself. The dividends of that investment were priceless.

Mastery has a powerful biological imperative. Athletes in sports see an increase in muscle "but also upon the ability of the nervous system to appropriately activate the muscles. Strength training may cause adaptive changes within the nervous system that allow a trainee to activate prime movers more fully in specific movements and to better coordinate the activation of all relevant muscles" (Sale 1988). More important than the muscular growth is the literal change in the structure of the brain.

The human mind is incredibly malleable and this is often an issue, especially for younger folk as bad parenting and guidance can lead many young people down unhealthy paths. The bright side is inculcating good habits and ingraining them into our neurons can change the trajectory of many lives.

A study in the *Journal of Preventative Medicine* from 2011 found young boys who played competitive sports had much better classroom behaviors. They found "such activity can affect attitudes and academic behavior, including enhanced concentration, attention, and improved classroom behavior" (Rasberry,2011). Another study Karmel Choi found "even after adjusting for BMI, employment status, educational attainment, and prior depression… higher levels of physical activity were associated with reduced odds of incident depression across all levels of genetic vulnerability, even among individuals at highest polygenic risk" (Choi, 2020). That means even children with high genetic predisposition to depression and mental health disorders saw improvements to their mental health thanks to sports.

Harnessing this biological imperative toward mastery is incredibly important for young men. A structured activity that allows them to grow and find value will translate to better behavioral outcomes.

Mastery is vital for bringing structure and order to one's life. Discipline is hard, but mastery makes it more attainable by giving one a reward system and the motivation to pursue it. If you follow a routine religiously, your life will be ordered and structured. You will be more productive than your undisciplined self. Mastery takes that to the next level by giving you a goal to work toward. Stagnation should never be the price of discipline because that makes for a rigid individual.

Mastery gives one hope for a better future. You can destroy a man by taking away his hope. What motivation is there to live if there is no promise of something more than subsistence, especially if that is all they have known? Mastery holds you accountable to your greater ideals. Everyone has a self-image, a personal narrative about their struggle. Mastery ensures we do our best to live as our best selves.

One nuance to understand about mastery is we can never grow complacent with its pursuit. The decline of coal country and the American Midwest present a cautionary tale on stagnation. An analysis from the *Milken Institute Review* notes how Midwest towns across the Appalachian Trail have fallen into disrepair. Coal used to the be the lifeblood of these communities, but over the past twenty years "fall in demand has contributed to a 28 percent decrease in total production and a 34 percent decline in coal-related employment" (Metcalf 2020). Towns and business built around coal and miners have been devastated due to rapid growth of natural gas and renewable energy. The skills miners spent generations cultivating became less valuable as the demands of the world changed.

Many miners found themselves on hard times and turned to drugs to deal with their depression. The article notes, "Deaths from drug overdoses have increased more than four-fold since 1999, rising to over 65,000 in 2018, with fatalities from opioid misuse far in the lead. Opioid mortality is geographically concentrated in the East Coast, Rust Belt and Southwest. And within the East, Appalachia has borne the brunt." Those are the consequences for men whose dedication to mastery is mishandled. Blindly investing in a skill is not mastery. Not all skills are equal, but any skill is valuable if used well. Miners expected to have the same jobs and consequent standards of living as their fathers before them, even though the world around them dramatically changed.

For mastery to survive, skill cannot be singularly focused. The jobs of the future require new skills and a new journey of mastery. It is not mastery to get better at digging coal, but to be dedicated to the craft of mining and finding new ways to innovate. While factories and mines closed in the Midwest and Rustbelt, startups opened their first websites in Silicon Valley. The mining industry is more productive than ever, but that is because of innovations made by scientists, engineers, and programmers, not miners. Without innovating, the miners lost their mastery over energy extraction and paid the price.

Innovation is an important touchstone for mastery. We need to constantly examine new perspectives to solve problems. Every time we encounter a barrier, we need to dedicate ourselves to overcoming it. Innovation must stay eclectic.

There are two types of mastery a masculine individual must consider: one avenue that creates competitive mastery, another that creates artistic mastery. Both are necessary to live a complete and fulfilling life as a man.

Competitive mastery is the dedication to a skill you can measure against someone else. Competitive mastery weaponizes the goals in your life and gives you the competitive drive to pursue excellence. Competition is an important aspect of masculinity because it provides men with objective benchmarks for their growth. Either they win, or they lose. There is an immediate consequence for failing to follow one's ambition.

While competition is important, not everything is competitive. Music is a great example because while there are different styles of competition that test out accuracy, creative interpretation, or improvisational skills, most experiences with music are far more intimate. It is an artform that allows the player to convey their will and emotions. Much like how improving ones vocabulary aides in conveying their thoughts, greater skill in the musical arts creates a space to better share emotions.

Teaching is also an artform, and Maicon doesn't always know when he's succeeding. Many people join the gym then leave. You can never know the exact reason why they left, whether they lost interest in the art, did not care for the vibe of the gym, or were just embarrassed because a small woman strangled them with ease.

Artistic mastery concerns itself with extending the capabilities of the individual. Progress is measured internally and creates a personalized sense of value. This provides an important emotional release because the only person you are competing against is yourself. Artistic mastery is a place to heal and reinvigorate yourself. The world will tear you down—that is something you must accept as a man. You will lose in the most humiliating and embarrassing ways possible. Artistic mastery is about giving yourself the space to channel your disappointment into productive energy.

A study on music class engagement found "children who attended class more regularly and had better classroom participation had stronger neural encoding of speech after 2 years of music training than did their less-engaged peers" (Kraus 2014). Playing instruments had the capacity to make students better communicators and listeners.

For some people that is public speaking, writing, music, or painting. It can be anything you want, but it must provide internal validation and benchmarks. It forces you to be responsible for yourself and never disappoint yourself.

Mastery provides the tools you need to control your destiny. There are too many distractions plaguing men, from social media to their own vices. They will win over you if you don't have the motivation to put yourself first. Mastery helps you reorient your life around healthy systems that prevent you from growing soft and comfortable. It gives you a way to prove yourself and stay valuable in society. Finding value as man is difficult—mastery is your salvation.

You must not fade away. You are a valuable being, but you must constantly invest in yourself, lest others decide your fate. Mastery is about agency, about giving you as much control over your life and creating value. Explore different skills and artforms and find ones that provide value and motivation for you. There should be at least one skill that provides competitive mastery, giving you the option to prove yourself to the world. There should be a skill that provides artistic mastery to give you the intrinsic motivation to move forward while also providing a place for you to express yourself and heal. Mastery will create value by helping you grow your talents and share them with the world. To respect yourself, you must master yourself.

CHAPTER 8

PRETTY LIES OF GAMBLING

———

I want to preface this chapter by introducing you, my reader, to a story—a story of stupidity in three parts. To begin, I offer you the story of my childhood best friend Wallace Rodriguez (an obviously fake name). He is an incredibly intelligent person, albeit very strange. He is genuinely one of the smartest people I know, but that has never stopped him from making an absolute fool of himself. In our junior year of high school, he nearly broke my finger with a mousetrap while working on a physics project. As of writing this book, I have yet to seek recompense for his carelessness, but that's a story for another time. In our senior year of high school, every student taking A.P. Economics in my school was enrolled in a stock market game. My friend Wallace took first place out of nearly three hundred students by turning $100,000 into over $640,000. I don't remember ever seeing him as smug as the day he hit his peak. I also don't remember seeing him more devastated than when he went from number one to last in the class by losing over a million dollars in the span of four hours.

His plan was to short—i.e. bet against—a stock. If the stock went down, he would make money, but if it went up, he would lose much more.

Another friend by the name of Daniel Cormier (a less fake name) also had the privilege of making a fool of himself in my presence, but with actual money. As avid mixed martial arts fans, we watched every major fight together during college. As a contest, we would make spreadsheets to store our pretend bets every fight card. The night of UFC 257: Poirier vs McGregor 2, he bet over two hundred dollars on the favorites of main and co-main event.

The main event was a thing of beauty. Bitter rivals, Dustin Poirier and Connor McGregor had previously faced off in 2014 where McGregor trounced Poirier in the first round—the culmination of weeks of trash talk and mental warfare. Many experts including myself and DC predicted the rematch to be no different than the first encounter, but we were dead wrong. Poirier weaponized a low calf kick to whittle away at McGregor's mobility. Conor was slow on the counters and spent much of his gas tank fighting takedowns. Poirier cornered McGregor against the cage and knocked him down. After a malicious ground-and-pound, the referee called a stop to the fight.

Between those two fights, Daniel lost over two hundred dollars and I felt the pain of his loss. The saddest part is I expected Daniel to know a lot better since he was studying mathematics and economics at a top twenty university. I warned him not to bet and even he knew it was the financially poor decision, but he was so emotionally invested in an outcome he threw all his education out the window.

The final, most recent story takes us back to Wallace. During the GameStop Corp. rally of 2021, he joined the army of retail investors from the subreddit r/WallStreetBets in driving up the price of distressed assets. Hedge funds like Melvin Capital took short positions on stocks like Game Stop and AMC. A few intelligent redditors caught wind of the scheme and used memes to drive the price of the stock, or "stonks" as they're known online. From the perspective of the hedge funds, these redditors were uncouth man-children living in their mothers' basements, sticking their head in a viper's den. From the perspective of the redditors, the rally represented a revolt against the financial elite who play by a different set of rules and extract wealth from the economy. From my perspective, both groups were filled with morons.

Wallace, a broke college student, threw his lot in with r/WallStreetBets and lost money. He bought GME at its peak and swallowed a tough pill when the stock cratered after "critics pointed out the hedge-fund contingent among Robinhood's own backers, [...] Sequoia Capital, a big beast of venture capital that led a $280m fundraising effort valuing Robinhood at $8.3bn in May 2020" (Davies, 2021). Both Sequoia and Robinhood have denied these claims as such actions would be highly illegal. Generally, to make a return on investment one must buy low and sell high. Four words, yet Wallace managed to get two of them wrong. He lost more than $160 to stock speculation, something I predicted would happen.

Wallace and Daniel had one thing in common, they gambled and lost. They aren't completely to blame—they were sold a lie too many people, disproportionately male, fall for. The lie of chance and fortune. To be a masculine man, you must build wealth, not squander it.

Time is money and unfortunately, the future is uncertain. There is a deep masculine urge to build wealth. My father for example, made it a priority his children would have assets left to them upon his passing and bought plots of land to celebrate the birth of each of his three children. Many young men grow up without this type of safety net and for fathers who can't provide it to their children, it's devastating.

Gambling is, in many ways, a coping mechanism for struggles in wealth creation. Everyone wants to get rich, but there are very few avenues to build fortunes sustainably and those doors close the lower one goes on the socio-economic ladder. Gambling tempts people who desperately want to change their futures with easy money and it often leads to ruin. It is a major threat to masculinity because it leads to financial catastrophe and a destruction of wealth.

Gambling is a serious issue, especially now there are online mediums to gamble. According to a paper by Gloria Wong at the US National Library of Medicine, gambling has been growing steadily in recent years. In 2001, only 42 percent of college students experimented with gambling but in 2011, 91 percent of young men (aged eighteen to twenty-five) engaged in gambling behaviors including card games, slot machines, and sports betting. Women were dipping into the scene at 86 percent of women surveyed. Wong writes social anxiety, a byproduct of financial insecurity, was one of "the significant mediators for gender differences in problems with gambling. Men took more risks and were more socially anxious than women, and greater risk-taking and more socially anxious individuals tended to have more problems with gambling" (Wong 2013). There was small but statistically significant difference between men and women when asked if they had gambled at all. The biggest difference occurred when the study asked about frequency of gambling.

While women tried gambling at comparable rates, the data seems to suggest the rush of gambling wasn't as rewarding for women and thus they didn't continue gambling after trying it. Of the young adults who attempt gambling activities men are more likely to become problem gamblers at 14 percent whereas of the women who attempted gambling only 3 percent went on to develop gambling addictions. The analysis dug deeper to find a reason why proclivities to gamble were nearly five times higher in men than women. The paper concluded gambling addiction had similar risk factors to other vices like alcohol, narcotics, and tobacco.

Women tended to be more risk-averse compared to men so the high from gambling tended to be less potent. Male competitive behaviors, the same that encourage binge drinking, also made the social high of winning a bit higher. Bragging rights are real motivators to do stupid things—gambling just happens to manifest the perfect conditions to do so. Men in that age group tended to have lower impulse control which correlated with higher rates of gambling addiction.

Gambling affects the brain's neurochemistry similarly to hard drugs like cocaine. Jabr Ferris writes in *Scientific American* in 2013 "continuous use of such drugs robs them of their power to induce euphoria. Addictive substances keep the brain so awash in dopamine that it eventually adapts by producing less of the molecule and becoming less responsive to its effects. As a consequence, addicts build up a tolerance to a drug, needing larger and larger amounts to get high." That tolerance rewires neural pathways in the prefrontal cortex, slowly chipping away at impulse-control and higher cognitive function. It is like rerouting a river. If the river flow is altered out of a body of water such as a lake, then that lake dries up over time. That lake being, in this instance, the prefrontal cortex.

Tolerance also leads down more destructive paths as Ferris elaborates, "research to date shows that pathological gamblers and drug addicts share many of the same genetic predispositions for impulsivity and reward seeking. Just as substance addicts require increasingly strong hits to get high, compulsive gamblers pursue ever riskier ventures. Likewise, both drug addicts and problem gamblers endure symptoms of withdrawal when separated from the chemical or thrill they desire. And a few studies suggest that some people are especially vulnerable to both drug addiction and compulsive gambling because their reward circuitry is inherently underactive—which may partially explain why they seek big thrills in the first place."

Male gambling addiction has far-reaching consequences. It can often manifest in destructive ways when there is a toxic environment that encourages this vice. Casinos famously block out natural light to create an isolation between the gambler and the outside world. You can't tell how many hours have passed as you slowly lose more and more of your money in a rigged game. Unfortunately, there is a double standard regarding what types of gambling are scorned. A day trader, wearing a bespoke suit with a Patek Philippe, engages in the same behavior but with more sophistication.

Wall Street functions exactly like a casino. In theory, there isn't supposed to be a house in the stock market, but the financial lobby has all but guaranteed institutional banking from the Federal Reserve and Congress: "Banks hire external lobbyists or set up in-house lobbying teams to meet privately with politicians and regulators in order to advance their interests. The financial sector spent $7.4 billion on lobbying from 1998 to 2016" (Dellis 2022).

The main difference between a casino and a Wall Street bank like Citigroup is scale. A casino may have a few million dollars circulating through it, but a bank moves trillions of dollars through the global financial network.

Scale is dangerous because it means there's spillover between personal and societal catastrophes. A man can gamble away his life savings, owe money to dangerous people, and find himself lying in a ditch if he lets his gambling problems spiral. If that man somehow finds himself in the financial capital of the world with billions at his fingertips, he can do more than harm just himself.

I was eight years old during the 2008 financial meltdown. At the time I didn't understand why so many businesses were shutting down, why my dad was more stressed by work, or even why most of the kids began picking on me. After studying economics and reading into the conditions, I understand more than ever why that period of my life was filled with so much darkness.

Mortgages were the lifeblood of the economy. Part of the American dream was working hard enough to save for your own home, a crucial step to building wealth. Unfortunately, deregulation and greed allowed a handful of shrewd and soulless bankers to weaponize mortgages.

"To qualify for a mortgage, you needed to meet certain criteria: a good FICO score (credit score), a stable income, and some form of down payment or collateral. Ideally you would only lend to people who had a high probability of paying back their loans. The safer they were, the lower their interest rate. One thing to note, mortgages were insured by the federal government. This policy had good intentions—if banks felt more secure in their investments, they'd lend more and more people would get home loans. Unfortunately, this created a moral hazard because banks could lend to riskier costumers knowing that they would be off the hook if they couldn't collect. That was bad enough, but there are levels to greed and bankers have true mastery in the art" (Wilber-May 2012).

Charles K. Wilber notes the importance of government regulation in the financial sector. Laws like the Glass–Steagall provisions prevented banks from over-leveraging themselves with depositor money. Unfortunately, "Since 1980, however, one of the main thrusts of public policy has been to free up markets by deregulation (including the repeal of the Glass–Steagall Act in 1999), cutting taxes and eliminating or reducing social programs." Both Republican and Democratic administrations have pursued these policies.

Banks sell debt all the time—that wasn't a new phenomenon. The innovation that fueled the subprime mortgage crisis were

Collateralized Debt Obligations. To understand CDOs, you need to understand tranches. Instead of selling the debt of one mortgage to you, what if I sold a portion of the debt, a tranche (French for slice)? CDOs were packages that bundled thousands of tranches from thousands of different mortgages. They were traded between banks and other financial institutions. At the same time, the even contrived asset known as a synthetic CDO or a CDO that contained tranches of other CDOs also gained popularity (Taibbi 2011). Ideally, these CDOs would have collapsed like the house of cards they were, but that didn't happen immediately. The reason why? Fraud.

Matt Taibbi of the *Rolling Stone* writes , "The Justice Department ends up leaning heavily on the SEC's army of 1,100 number-crunching investigators to make their cases." That disconnect made regulation of fraud increasingly difficult. The first ones to start slipping were the credit rating agencies.

There are three big credit rating agencies: Moody's, Standard & Poor's, and Fitch. Their job is to analyze the integrity of securities like bonds, stocks, and even CDOs. Ideally, they protect investors by giving some objective transparency regarding the risk of securities. Unfortunately, they wore their corruption on their sleeves. No person in their right mind should rate a CDO AAA (the best). Banks pumped the tranches with bad loans to the point of creating a financial ticking timebomb. Unfortunately, there was another moral hazard. You had to pay a credit agency for your rating; if you didn't like the result, you just took it to a different agency. This was pay to play fraud, plain and simple.

The result of BBB (the absolute worst) CDOs getting an AAA rating was the creation of an asset with a guaranteed failure.

The next level of fraud involved shorting these assets. Generally, when you buy a security you hope for its market value to go up, increasing your wealth. Shorting is betting against that security to profit when it goes down in the market. If I wanted to short Apple stocks, I would borrow the stocks from an investor, sell immediately, then wait for the stock to drop. I am contractually obligated to buy back the stock so I may suffer greatly if the stock spikes.

When Melvin Capital and other hedge funds shorted Game Stop, they did so when the stock lingered in the single digits. The r/WallStreetBets rally pushed the stock to a record high of greater than $430. Because a stock can grow infinitely, one's losses when shorting can be infinite. If I buy $10,000 of Apple stock, the most I can lose is that $10,000. If I short the stock and it grows by ten times, I lose $100,000.

Bankers and managers on Wall Street marketed the CDO as a safe investment to pension funds and other banks. They would turn around and short those same CDOs to fail, which they inevitably did. They made money on the selling and speculation. When the CDOs failed, as they did in early 2008, the banks and funds caught holding the bag failed. Lehman Brothers was the first big name to collapse, followed by Bear Stearns, Morgan Stanley, and so on. Due to years of deregulation regarding bank size and speculation, banks were too big to fail. That meant, if they failed, the shockwave would paralyze then suffocate the rest of the economy.

Charles Wilber further explains, "The insurance industry calls this a moral hazard. A person who buys auto theft insurance, for example, has less incentive to be careful, say, by locking the car doors. If the car is stolen, the insurance company will compensate. Likewise, bank executives will be tempted to take on more risk than is prudent when they know they will be bailed out by government, as they were in the most recent financial crisis" (Wilber-May, 2012).

The government was left in a position where they bailed out the banks to preserve some stability in the system. Unfortunately, they didn't do enough for regular people and so began waves of job loss and home foreclosures.

The hedge funds were clearly in the wrong. Speculative behavior is gambling. Betting on whether a stock rises or dives is no different than betting on horse race. Once again, the difference is scale. The case for hedge funds is the belief they are riskier ventures for sophisticated investors who seek greater returns on their assets. That bullshit isn't backed up by the data. According to Hedgeweek, a news organization that tracks Wall Street, over the past ten years the S&P 500—an average return on stock—was about 14 percent per year, but hedge funds only returned 8 percent per year (HedgeWeek 2020). Now the standard deviation across the different funds was far greater than within the S&P 500, meaning the top hedge funds did incredibly well, but that isn't an argument in favor of them. Finding the right hedge fund becomes another exercise in gambling and speculation.

I have a theory the most functional problem gamblers find their way into the top hedge funds and banks. Former hedge fund correspondent for the *Financial Times*, Lindsay Fortado, notes, "Women control less than 1 per cent of the $3tn in assets managed in the hedge fund industry. Male portfolio managers outnumber women by 20 to one" (Fortado 2017). We could handwave away some of this disparity by pointing out far fewer women work in the financial industry, but that isn't the whole picture.

Women—in the vein of being far more risk sensitive—showed higher returns on the assets they managed. This is unsurprising. In a system where gambling is a lose-lose situation, the people who gamble less do much better.

This trend coincides with social media financial influencers. Their whole shtick is giving people the generic advice to "build passive income." At face value, they are just guiding young men on the importance of building wealth. That's a sentiment I can get behind wholeheartedly. Unfortunately, this isn't coming from the goodness of their hearts. Most of the time these influencers are just grifters feeding their impressionable audience to their ridiculous wealth building programs and seminars. Most of these programs are excellent ways to burn money. I can't think of any worse use of money than paying so-called sophisticated investors to build wealth. If hedge funds who hire professionals can't consistently beat the market, hoping random influencers would surpass them is a stretch.

Most of the time, these are just scams that push people to pay for more seminars. I don't believe in these grifters and I find it annoying they manipulate young men who are already worried about money into parting with more of their cash.

One of the reasons why men are compelled to following finance gurus—whether it be into betting, retail investing, hedge funds—is because there is a very real concern with financial security. One of the most important tenets of being a man is creating a nest. It's the capability to support one's self and in the future, a family. Before, a man with a strong back could find a job at a local steel mill with limited education and earn a decent middle-class lifestyle. Because of changing roles in the economy, those jobs are disappearing. I am not surprised in this uncertainty where young men cannot follow in the footsteps of their fathers, they seek ancillary forms of income especially if they don't succeed in school.

The number of young men in my generation who have "Entrepreneur" in their social media bio is astounding. If they were starting businesses in revolutionary fields, we would solve all of the world's problems. Unfortunately, many ventures are limited to sneaker reselling or drop shipping. It is possible to make money in those fields, but their value is dubious.

The goal of a side hustle is to be a venue for a person to follow their dreams. Many pet projects turn into works of art, small businesses, or inventions. In a world where every teacher must also drive Ubers or rent out their spare bedroom on Airbnb, it's no wonder young men are more desperate to make some sort of money that's divorced from their nine-to-five.

One solution on the individual level is skill building. As mentioned previously, mastery is an essential component of masculinity, one reason being it has the potential to create value outside of one's expertise. I offer myself as an example. In addition to writing this book, I have devoted time to completing certificates in cybersecurity. In 2019 there were more than one hundred thousand unfilled cybersecurity positions, some of which didn't even ask for a four-year degree. Building skills in that area gives me at best a stable career path and at worst a decent fallback. I personally hate technology, but I understand the necessity of creating skills in that field. In addition, I took classes in Python and Java to augment my understanding of cybersecurity and pad my resume. Rather than investing in the illusory stock or crypto currency markets, I choose to invest in myself. I suggest you, my reader, do the same.

One solution from a public policy perspective are universal programs like a universal basic income, a federal works program, and universal healthcare (sometimes called single-payer). Universal programs are important because they create a very necessary social safety net that empowers individuals to climb higher.

A universal basic income complementing other benefits sets a floor that allows people more flexibility in their work. It's hard to spend time to work on yourself when you have eighty-hour work weeks just to keep a roof over your head. A study from Finland showed promising results. The study found "that a basic income actually had a positive impact on employment. People on the basic income were more likely to be employed than those in the control group, and the differences were statistically significant" (Allas, 2021). The researchers explained this was the result of younger people taking more time to get trained and educated so they could apply for better paying jobs.

Stockton, California is another example. NPR notes the UBI pilot program of $500 a month "increased recipients' full-time employment by 12 percentage points and decreased their measurable feelings of anxiety and depression, compared with their control-group counterparts" (Treisman, 2021). The most astounding result was the fact "individuals spent most of the money on basic needs, including food, merchandise, utilities and auto costs, with less than 1 percent going toward alcohol and/or tobacco." A universal basic income made people more responsible with their money and decreased their vices.

A federal jobs guarantee gives young men in poorer communities with limited job opportunities an important stepping-stone to build their futures. One of the paradoxes of modern employment is most jobs require prior experience, but the only way to get experience is with a job in the first place. In the United States, there already exists a rudimentary form of a jobs guarantee called the military. Imagine if there was an expansion of jobs, say under a Green New Deal or New New Deal that gave men jobs as easily as the military gives them rifles. It would go a long way to fix the massive instability caused by movements in the economy.

Finally, there is a need for a robust healthcare system. One major downside of employer-tied health care is entrepreneurs are disincentivized from leaving their job to start their own business since they will lose their health coverage. This dilemma becomes even more serious when that person has a dependent. A Harris Poll found "54 percent of Americans say they've delayed care for themselves in the past year because of cost, and another 23 percent delayed care for more than a year for the same reason. Meanwhile, 10 percent of Americans with children under the age of 18 have delayed care for a dependent or child because of financial issues" (Carter, 2013). That system is not conducive to effective public health.

One of the benefits of a universal healthcare system is patients see their doctors regularly rather than only right after a health scare because of the cost of care. This allows doctors to help patients with more preventative care that saves dividends in the future. In a world where we treat preventative care with the utmost gravity, we can catch early signs of gambling addiction and give treatment to the young men who need it.

Ideally, these policies make it easier for men to build futures. Futures where they can get married if they want to, have children if they want to, start a business if they want to. The goals are to replace speculation and gambling with stable wealth creation.

Fixing the vice of gambling requires steps on the individual and public policy level—we can't rely on just one solution. We understand men are more susceptible to gambling than women and economic stresses are compounding the issue. To help young men, from Daniel and Wallace to the socially awkward redditors at r/WallStreetBets to even the finance bros at investment banks, we need to encourage young men to rid themselves of their chains and push forward for financial security.

CHAPTER 9

CULT OF VANITY

———

If you, my reader, spent enough time in front of your mirror, you could find a myriad of flaws in your physical appearance. Your grievances with your appearance may include jawline sharpness, nose shape, eye width, acne, receding hairline, or body composition. We are imperfect beings; many parts of us are asymmetric and unaesthetic. Ideally, we acknowledge our physical flaws and move on with our lives, but many young men obsess over their faults and spend too much time bemoaning their misfortune. This obsession is a product of vanity.

Vanity is conventionally defined as the excessive admiration of one's physical appearance, but its opposite also holds true. The obsessive self-criticism of one's physical defects is also vain because it similarly conflates one's worth with their appearance. One's human value cannot be constrained or defined by their looks. Such thinking is shallow and vapid. One's attractiveness doesn't directly predict their success or their value. There are indeed advantages to being conventionally good looking, but that's all they are, advantages.

Vanity presents an interesting obstacle for men because men are dominated by the visual. Beauty and sex appeal in a woman matter far more to a man than for a woman in a man. This is one reason why men exceed women in the consumption of pornography and why men outnumber women on dating apps like Tinder (Tyson 2016). Many men will stare at a woman's curves even if he is in a committed relationship with a different woman. The visual is powerful, but when it becomes the sole power, it becomes destructive.

When a man directs his vanity inward, he begins sundering his being. To a vain person, any imperfection is a potential threat. If one's value is tied to one's visual aesthetic, then every defect is indicative of some great character failing. These imperfections become the vain man's primary concern, leading to an ultimatum: the deficiency should be exorcised lest the individual deem themselves invalid. When these thoughts of inadequacy fester in young men's minds, they open the avenue to a severe illness called Body Dysmorphia Disorder.

According to the American Psychological Association, "Body Dysmorphia Disorder is a mental illness where the subject deals with an excessive and obsessive focus on appearance flaws." The operative terms are excessive and obsessive. A man wanting to reduce the size of his love handles may choose to run more in the mornings; it's not a drastic decision that changes his behavioral pattern. A man spending hours in front of the mirror measuring the diameter of the folds of fat with calipers, taking harmful steroids, and running to the point of serious injury to his knees is a prime example of a victim of body dysmorphia. This obsession upends the second man's entire life, whereas the former has seen a moderate improvement in his life.

Unfortunately, men are locked in a race to the bottom in the field of body dysmorphia. Over the past twenty-five years, the rate of body dysmorphia has tripled in men to 43 percent, rivaling women. Vanity, once considered a womanly vice, is just as expansive in men as women. Men are usually concerned with acne or scarring, hair thinning, nose size or shape, and genitals (Philips 2001). There are two emerging problems with body dysmorphia in men: the rampant underdiagnosis of the affliction and the difficulty in finding an effective treatment. To treat a mental illness regarding body image, a psychiatrist or doctor cannot handwave away the problem with elective surgery: "There needs to be a comprehensive treatment plan that will vary between individuals. The need grows greater each day because body dysmorphia in men is rising rapidly" (Philips 2001).

Before talking about its impacts, we need to understand why the male body dysmorphia is on the rise. This phenomenon's central driving force is social media, which promotes unrealistic bodily expectations of beauty and aesthetics.

South Korea is an interesting microcosm for this. K-pop is the quintessential Korean export, but it forms a symbiotic relationship with two other industries: cosmetics and plastic surgery. The band BTS "is producing—along with hit songs—a whopping $4.65 billion of gross domestic product" (Pesek 2019). They are globally popular and they help grow the Korean cosmetics industry which exports $7.6 billion to the US alone. In a digital world, culture is directed by digital media. Pop idols, both men and women, promote cosmetic products while contractually bound to undergo plastic surgery to maintain their image. Many of these contracts are predatory in nature and turn the idol's body into a menagerie of unattainable beauty. There is an implicit statement made by Korean record companies, makeup boutiques, and plastic surgeons that talent belongs to the beautiful. These messages reach far beyond media. Many middle-aged men are jumping on the plastic surgery bandwagon because of the prevailing belief looking younger and healthier improves their market value. Intuitively that makes sense. In a country where the population is aging and it is a requirement to post a recent picture of oneself on a resume, it may be reasonable to prioritize a youthful candidate who may work longer and harder. While this deliberation is undoubtedly ageist, it is a real conversation in Korean hiring. It becomes much more likely one obsesses over their own appearance if their society points out their faults at every given opportunity.

The dating game also contributes to the growth of vanity in men. With the rise of dating apps like Tinder and Bumble, one's image becomes even more valuable. In a visual medium, the best aesthetics succeed. Tinder exacerbates this problem by purposefully discriminating against men. It is unsurprising Tinder has a gender gap in its user base. Male users outnumber female users nine to one, creating a challenging environment for heterosexual men. Tinder takes this disparity to the next level by placing an algorithm that ranks men's profiles (Tyson 2016). A social ranking algorithm is inherently problematic because it doesn't give a level playing field between men. On average, women get sixteen times more frequent matches than men, and Tinder's whole business model is based on getting men to pay for premium features to get noticed. Yet another facet of late-stage capitalism, Tinder profits out of making young men feel inadequate and lonely. Tinder has convinced young men the reason they can't find success in meeting young women is their optics are lacking. This perception feeds into anxiety and all but ensures a sizeable position of male users will develop anxiety around their self-image.

Anxiety and depression, born of vanity, have profoundly dangerous implications for the health of young men. No one would bat an eye if the worst effect of rising body dysmorphia in men were the rise in dating app popularity at the cost of lighter wallets. Unfortunately, men are not that banal. When one is upset with their body, and that irritation becomes obsessive, they take drastic actions.

It is hard to criticize a healthy diet and exercise. Done well, they can improve a person's body composition, mental health, and vitality. Unfortunately, when young men obsess over their physical features, modest gains aren't enough (Phillipou 2021). Some men will bargain with themselves, foregoing expensive plastic surgery by compensating with their physique. On one level, that's admirable, but if one's vanity is focused on one physique, the obsession can lead to a different and deadlier mental illness known as bigorexia.

Bigorexia is the mirror to anorexia nervosa, where instead of getting skinnier, the patient—mostly men—focuses on getting bigger by increasing muscularity and vascularity. This is a profoundly serious condition because, in a classic masculine fashion, it can be much more destructive than its feminine counterpart. Young men obsessed with getting bigger will adopt extreme diets, suffer overuse injuries in the gym, and experiment with image and performance-enhancing drugs (IPEDs) like laxatives and anabolic-androgenic steroids. I cannot stress how dangerous these are to a young person's health. They have been proven to do irreparable damage to the endocrine system, increase chances of cardiac arrest, and have claimed the lives of so many men (Morris 2018). In the United Kingdom, over one million men were found to use IPEDs for the sole purpose of aesthetics, not athletics. That is over 3 percent of the male population. It is one conversation when professional athletes use IPEDs in careers with millions of dollars at stake, and it becomes another when a fourteen-year-old boy uses them to keep up with his friends also using them. There isn't even an argument for material benefit coming from using IPEDs for aesthetics, but their use is growing.

It is deeply upsetting there are children who hurt themselves to emulate the physiques of superhero movie stars, many of whom also use IPEDs when preparing for their roles. Rich actors can afford expensive treatment for their steroid use, and an unsophisticated teenager cannot. I also want to lay blame on the sport of bodybuilding and social media influencers who use their unnatural physiques to market to impressionable young children. They're grifters who either lie about their steroid use or shamelessly promote it.

Sharp jawlines and giant muscles are not the totality of masculinity. On the contrary, an insecure young man hurting himself to prove his validation is the exact opposite of confident masculinity. It takes tremendous strength and wisdom to accept one's limitations. Some people are limited by genetics and biomechanics for how much muscle their body can support naturally. Most people will never reach their genetic limits, but a real man doesn't spend his days complaining about his poor genetics or mutilating himself out of spite.

To fix one's vanity, there needs to be a radical realignment of one's priorities and an authentic understanding of beauty. One's beauty should be a byproduct of their value as a human being. If aesthetic is the center piece, then one may neglect the other components necessary to live a fulfilling life. If someone lives a healthy life, then they will be rewarded.

Athletes are a great example of how having aesthetics exists as a byproduct. Many boxers are shredded with six-packs and defined chests. Many don't spend time in front of the gym mirror doing bicep curls. They train for their sport, optimize their diet for performance, and take much-needed rest for recovery. They don't covet the physique; the physique follows their desire for a greater purpose.

Not everyone should be a boxer—and the sport's incredible rate of brain damage makes it a tough sell for excellence—but the notion still stands: chase greatness, not aesthetics. The musculature is appealing to both men and women because it signifies a man is capable and strong. If you build the muscle in lieu of the strength and skill, then you undermine the very system of human adaptation.

There is an understanding of beauty in the modern world that beauty is perfection. Airbrushed and photoshopped models on magazine covers are what French philosopher and sociologist Jean Baudrillard would define in 1994 as simulacra, copies without an original: "The media represents a world that is more real than reality that we can experience. People lose the ability to distinguish between reality and fantasy. They also begin to engage with the fantasy without realizing what it really is. They seek happiness and fulfillment through the simulacra of reality, e.g. media and avoid the contact/inter-action with the real world."

A picture is a copy of a person. It isn't an authentic replication of the object because the world is four-dimensional with an x, y, z, and time axis to show the entirety of the subject. A photograph is two-dimensional, meaning a lot of the object is cut out and distorted. It falls on the beholder to perceive depth and to draw their own conclusions on the essence (meaning) of the picture. When the photographer manipulates the photo with special lighting, distortion, or computer editing, they further distort the image. A fitness influencer taking a photo with a post-workout pump, flattering angle, and perfect lighting is showing an image that can only exist at one point in time. It is by no means the baseline or even natural impression of the person. A system that deals in simulacra isn't real, it is hyperreal.

Baudrillard, a man far ahead of his time, had stark warnings for hyperreal societies. The very concept of reality is shaped by skewed images. The only antidote to hyperreality is authenticity. If you met the model from the cover of *Glamour*, you'd notice the mole on her arm, the stray hairs hinting at a uni-brow, or the laziness of her eyes. Likewise, you'd be drawn in by her laugh, marvel at her knowledge of economics, or shed a tear as she recounts her story of escaping violence in Serbia.

The authentic value of a person isn't depicted in a photograph. The photographs suppress the true value of human beings. It is our vanity that blinds us to our virtues. A person living a fulfilling and healthy life will create an authentic beauty no camera could ever understand, much less capture.

Competitive bodybuilding could never understand this concept. Bodybuilding without steroids is rare, so rare one could consider it extinct. Bodybuilders commit the heinous crime of turning themselves into simulacra. The sport punishes natural athletes and coerces them into taking IPEDs. There is a vague idea of the perfect Adonis, and if a competitor reaches those perfect proportions, then they have ascended into divinity. Unfortunately, the only people who benefit from this ideal are niche subculture, mostly men, that worships or "stans" these athletes in an almost homoerotic ritual. Bodybuilders are inferior to other athletes or even hobbyists because their value exists outside of their control. If they lose their followers and competitions, they are left with hollow images. In an arena where anyone can look like an athlete, only the ones who can perform like one gain respect.

If some people enjoy looking big in the mirror, then more power to them, but this obsessive and self-destructive vanity helps no one and harms everyone it touches. Your dedication to self-improvement must elevate you physically, emotionally, socially, mentally, and spiritually. The obsession sparked by vanity weaponizes the inherent and virtuous drive for personal growth into a vehicle fueled by insecurity. A man's dedication to his personal grooming, physique, and looks should elevate him and not come at the cost of his well-being.

To live authentically, men must enjoy the beauty of their struggles, their failures, and their flaws. It is not an easy thing to do, and it requires no small modicum of maturity and wisdom.

You must have your cause be greater than the validation of good looks. Work toward something that can't be quantified in the mirror. If you're a sprinter, focus on shaving time off your hundred-meter sprint. As you develop your skills, enjoy the rush of accomplishment that comes by beating your previous best. When you face a slump, you can always look down at your shredded and powerful legs and take pride in how far you have come.

You must work with your unideal features, not hide them. If your hair is falling out prematurely due to a genetic predisposition to male pattern baldness, consider shaving it clean. A shiny dome matched with a confident smile will do a lot to impress the ladies and gentlemen in the crowd. It sends a powerful message about the strength of one's character when they lean into their uniqueness.

You must present your best self. There's nothing wrong with combing your hair before picture day. We must play by the rules of society until we are skillful enough to break them. It is important we present our best selves to others, not only out of courtesy to them but out of respect to one's self. If you are unhappy with yourself, then no amount of exercise, dieting, plastic surgery, or steroids will make you happy. None of those things will give you confidence or fulfillment if you lack either of the latter in the first place.

You must love and accept yourself. The adage rings true. No one will love you until you love yourself. No one will respect you until you respect yourself. Vanity is not self-love; it is self-objectification. Vanity is the reductionist view one's self is valuable for their beauty. This book advocates self-love is loving one's entirety. That is a difficult thing to do. It takes deep introspection and an accurate assessment of one's character.

In conclusion, one must be vigilant against vanity. Vanity is a shallow and vacuous understanding of self-worth. It will breed insecurity regarding one's body image, leading to body dysmorphia and mental health problems. In the modern world, young men are more at risk than ever. For a growing young man and the community that supports him, understanding how to spot the early signs and combat them is of the utmost importance. To avoid or overcome vanity, one must live authentically.

Living authentically means drawing value from all of one's facets. The components of someone's lifestyle must elevate them, not drag them to the bottomless pits of despair. Living authentically means having a more significant cause that looks beyond one's vanity, wearing one's flaws like armor, understanding the nature of one's own happiness, and genuinely loving oneself. These components of your lifestyle must elevate you. They should never constrain you, and more importantly, they should never define you.

CHAPTER 10

PEACE OF SUFFERING

———

You can tell a lot about a man by reading his hands. I am not talking about horoscopes; I mean the actual structure and form of his hand. A weightlifter has mountainous callouses on the mounds of his fingers, a judoka has burned callouses above his cleanly cut fingernails, and a surgeon's delicate hands will carry a strict discipline and economy of movement unmatched by martial artists. A man should bear his hands with pride, for they tell a more in-depth story of his struggle than any tale he could spin.

Your suffering will change you on the molecular level. Children who grew up in abusive families have unique development of their brain structures, which will stick with them for the rest of their lives. We fixate a lot on visible scars, but mental scars are just as unique. A study in the *American Journal of Preventative Medicine* found increased exposure to childhood trauma "had 4- to 12-fold increased health risks for alcoholism, drug abuse, depression, and suicide attempt; a 2- to 4-fold increase in smoking, poor self-rated health, ≥ 50 sexual intercourse partners, and sexually transmitted disease; and a 1.4- to 1.6-fold increase in physical inactivity and severe obesity" (Felitti 1998).

To develop one's own masculinity, one must learn to handle their trauma. No society, however advanced, can perfectly shield all children. We must learn to embrace our own suffering to live with ourselves. The Japanese have a term called *kintsugi*, which explores this concept. Whenever valuable pottery breaks, instead of throwing it out, there is a tradition of mending the vessel with gold and lacquer. The belief is after something has shown its damage, it becomes more beautiful because of its unique story.

The practice of *kintsugi* can teach us an important lesson. Damage does not have to be permanent. Our trauma is no different than the pottery's, but the distinction is we can heal ourselves.

An important lesson is one should not be so enamored by their own suffering it blinds them to others' suffering.

It's essential to take a look at historical figures and understand their strengths and weaknesses to replicate or avoid. Joe Biden, the fourty-sixth President of the United States, comes a rich history of struggles and triumphs, as well as blunders and missteps. Joe Biden is a complicated man.

But he is not a perfect man, and I don't believe there is such a thing as an ideal man. So let's look at him in his entirety and understand just how powerful his ability to connect with other people is. Joe Biden grew up as Scranton Joe. He was a working-class kid. An article chronicling his past notes "as a child, Joe Jr. suffered from a severe stutter. He endured bullies and the shame that accompanies the affliction. Kindergarten speech therapy did not work so he decided to fight his battle on his own" (Levingston 2021).

But he persevered. He was incredibly compelling as an individual; he was able to make friends, connect with people on deeper levels. Even though he didn't go to top Ivy League schools, he succeeded in becoming a senator from Delaware.

His triumph was followed by his greatest loss. Six weeks after he won the election, his wife "set out to do some Christmas shopping with the three kids when a tractor trailer plowed into her station wagon, killing his wife Neilia and daughter Naomi. Beau and Hunter were badly injured. Biden considered giving up his Senate seat before he even arrived, but Democratic and Republican colleagues persuaded him to give the new job a try" (Levingston 2021).

For lesser men, this loss would have broken them. But Joe Biden used that pain to connect with other people. He was a massive player in politics in Washington DC, working with people who we by all accounts would consider monsters today to get bills passed.

But he has a very human connection. Right before he went to the *New York Times* for an interview for the publication's nomination, he went up the elevator. It was chauffeured by a woman named Jacquelyn Brittany.

In a quote from her: "I take powerful people up my elevator all the time [...] In a short time, I spent with Joe Biden, and I could tell he really saw me even [...] when he went into his important meeting. [...] He takes my story with him. Joe Biden has room in his heart for more than just himself" (Linskey 2020).

That's powerful. Many people go through tragedy in life, and become callous to the suffering of others. A father who has seen the horrors of war may have a difficult time connecting with a son who is dealing with bullies at school. It's not he doesn't think his son is dealing with a problem; he just doesn't believe that problem is that serious because he went through something much worse.

That's a very myopic view because we all have different capabilities and different strengths. You are going to go through different struggles than someone else. That doesn't mean your efforts matter less.

Joe Biden clearly displays an understanding of charisma that is built on empathy. While sharing one's trauma to process it carries considerable benefits to the individual, it also has many external benefits.

Joe Biden is able to connect with people. There are limitations he has, but there is an important ability you can learn from him, which is learn to see people from where they come from.

Everyone is coming from different angles from different positions with different perspectives. Joe Biden, at the very least, can offer people dignity. At his lowest point, he knew who he was. And I firmly believe you know who you are at your lowest point. Joe Biden's inherent connection with other people traces back to his ability to see people from where they come from.

He has his own problems. He has his own blind spots, but who doesn't? There is something vital you can learn from Biden.

He can connect with people, even people who are opposed to him, because he doesn't let his pain dictate his life. We inherit trauma passed down from parent to child. Children who were beaten by their parents are more likely to become violent and in turn beat their children in the future.

We inherit the bad habits of the people who raised us. My grandfather had a great quote: "You can either remember the pain. Or you can remember the suffering." If you choose to remember the struggles you faced, and how hurt you are all the time, you're going to become bitter.

My grandfather was often the target of verbal abuse in my family. His name was mentioned in more than a few curses because he was an abrasive person. He relentlessly pestered his siblings, cousins, and children. He was incredibly reliable, but very demanding. He would often barge into homes and make demands. He would not stop pestering you until you gave him what he wanted. One summer, he dragged me across the streets of Bangalore on his motorcycle to find and fit a Nehru jacket. It was incredibly uncomfortable, but I knew better than to pick a fight with him.

The jacket was ugly and I quickly outgrew it, but it was his way of showing his love for me. That same summer, my passport expired and he moved mountains to gather the paperwork to get it renewed. He bribed police officers, cozied up with bureaucrats, and even forged a fake address to return me home. It was risky, but he moved mountains all because my mother asked him for help.

It wasn't until after his death members of my family realized how important he was to all of us. People used to curse him and the chaos he caused, but they never stopped to ask how that might have hurt him. I believe I always treated him with love and respect, but I can't definitively know. My grandfather never let himself get hurt by the people around him. In the latter years of his life, he lost vision in one eye and the use of 70 percent of his arteries and veins because of diabetes.

We pleaded with and yelled at him to take his health seriously, and he would acquiesce for a few days before sneaking candy bars into my pocket while my mother wasn't looking. If I got in trouble, he would cause a scene so everyone would scold him instead of me.

The day before he passed away, he drove his motorcycle through rush hour traffic in search of the sweetest mangoes. He lived like a king. He passed away in his sleep peacefully. He died like a king. He could have been bitter over how he was treated, but he chose to look past his suffering and empathize with everyone around him.

He taught me if you are so enamored by your own suffering you cannot see the struggles of another person, you are no different than the people who caused your own suffering. Trauma is intergenerational and infectious. Failing to deal with trauma will manifest that trauma on others, especially the ones you are closest to.

If you remember the pain and understand how debilitating it was, you won't repeat that on another person. Remembering is important in connecting with other people. You must be honest about your struggles, your pain, and your rage, if you ever want to connect with someone else.

One prescription this book can give for all men is to seek therapy from a mental health professional. It might be a tall ask, especially if these services are expensive in your region, but I ask you see it as an investment. A longitudinal study out of the UK found "that men experienced an increase of 13% in their income within the next year after consulting psychotherapy services" (Contoyannis 2001). Researchers found men who could process trauma were more productive and far happier and that translated perfectly into greater earnings.

Unfortunately, men seemed hesitant to seek out these services. The paper noted while "approximately 23% of women entered into therapy, only 15% of men" sought treatment. Trained professionals often have the insight to deal with trauma and help men recover, but it is the responsibility of men to take the first step to confront trauma.

With complete remorse and acceptance, men must talk about their pain and suffering on an emotional level. That will make it easier for other people to communicate with him. Because if you can take the first step and talk to someone about your pain, you create a safe space for them to share. And I think once we see each other in our lowest of lows, we can better understand each other.

Men have been taught to repress their trauma and that has always been a recipe for disaster. Problems do not go away. They can be repressed for a time, but they always come back. Modern masculinity requires men to stand up for themselves by tackling their trauma head on.

CHAPTER 11

REIGN OF KING

———

The most impactful leaders of all time were strong men; they were shrewd, intelligent, and wise. They were very strong-willed. This is something we have to analyze because will-power is a very foundational part of masculinity. Unlike confidence, it's unwavering. It is a precursor to build skill because unless you are ready to power through difficult problems, you will not overcome them.

Kaiser Wilhelm II is an excellent example of where pride builds a negative synergy with willpower. He inherited the German Empire from his father, Kaiser Wilhelm I. Wilhelm II might have been the leader, the head of state, but he was not the man who built Germany. That credit goes to Otto von Bismarck, whose shrewd and cunning tactics combined with his incredible force and will, united a nation that was divided for thousands of years.

Both Bismarck and the Kaiser were incredibly willful people, but unlike the Kaiser, Bismarck was shrewd and calculating. Kaiser Wilhelm—scared of Bismarck—dismissed him, forgoing his last advice and ultimately dooming the German

Empire. Bismarck advised the Kaiser to avoid making enemies of Russia and Britain. Two easy steps he could have taken were to renew the joint declarations with Russia and avoid a naval build up that could threaten Britain.

The Kaiser failed on both counts and alienated both powers. The irony is through his grandmother, Queen Victoria of Britain, he had familial connections to Russia and most other monarchs in Europe. Wilhelm II's reign was set up by his father and Bismarck to be an era of German prosperity, but he squandered it by alienating potential allies. He was dedicated to German superiority, but his refusal to listen to sage advice doomed the empire. His willfulness became stubbornness and that stubbornness reaped destruction.

When I think about the most adamant will I have ever met, I can't help but think about my grandfather. He was the most masculine presence I ever knew, and I credit that to his unwavering will. It was tough to tell him to stop when he had made up his mind to do something. Once he had started a venture, he would move the world to make sure he would get his way. He knew how to express himself and never showed shame.

He is the same man who would go to work dressed up as a South Indian mobster, then the next day, a crisp suit and tie. He presented himself exactly as he felt, without any pretenses or façades. My grandfather lived like a king and subsequently died like a king.

He knew how to live dangerously at seventy-one years old. He would drive through the crowded traffic of Bangalore while blind in one eye. He treated people respectfully, but never out of subservience. The first thing he did after he moved into his old house right across from a police station was befriend the police chief. That is relationship building. He got away with many illegal things because of his ability to court people and form good relationships.

In a developing country like India, those skills were necessary to ensure prosperity. If the game is dirty, you must play dirty. In the long run, it came back to bite him, but he was a results first man.

He was scrappy and always found a way to bounce back. He started multiple businesses, mostly because the previous ones went out of business. Every time something went wrong for him, every time he struggled, he would always find a way to make money. He still found a way to bounce back. And for a Brahmin, that's a very rare trait.

Brahmins were expected to follow safe and learned lifestyles. One of my grandfather's sisters was among the first women to earn a PhD in India. They were a privileged class and were expected to be reserved and conservative in their mannerisms. My grandfather fit no such archetype.

He was fearless, and he didn't worry about the future; neuroticism was an unheard of concept for him. It wasn't just that he was an optimist. For him, there was no such thing as a negative outcome. He was always on top of things. He was dependable. His word was as good as law.

Understanding my grandfather is vital for understanding willpower because what gave him strength also created a multitude of problems for him in his old age as he was falling apart. He became a victim of his vices.

His willpower was the cornerstone of his conception of masculinity. To break another's will, one's own will must be unbreakable. If you are strong, the world will move around you. When shit hits the fan and the world starts falling apart, people will start following the one person who has the right answers. And my grandfather, always confident, so always willful of his actions, will always be that figure. If you have a strong will, you will break the wills of other people in an argument. You'll never wilt. And if you have a strong will people who have weaker wills will follow you.

Chael Sonnen recounts the story of Dan Gable, an Olympic wrestler and NCAA Division One athlete. Gable was the icon for weaponizing pace to break opponents. Sonnen notes "the idea that I will work harder than you at any given point, to the point where you will be so exhausted you quit a fight, ends when a person cannot defend themselves. And if you are tired, you are not going to bring up your hands to defend yourself" (2020). Dan Gable weaponized his pace with the belief. If you outwork your opponent, you will make them give up. It is quite literally a testament of your will versus theirs.

In both personal and competitive endeavors, the bottleneck is willpower. There will always be a battle of wills, be it your own against a rival or against your own will to give up. An understanding of masculinity will require an understanding of this battle.

And willpower is the precursor to confidence and charisma. If everyone calls you crazy and stupid, but you stick to your guns, you're able to tell people you will stand for what's right. Even if you have to stand alone, that's very compelling. A cornered animal is terrifying because it is willing to do whatever is necessary. That willpower, that strength is not something people ignore.

It takes great strength to think yourself right when everyone says you're wrong. Likewise, it is the height of stupidity to never admit it when you are wrong. You must find a balance in this. When someone realizes they're wrong, the initial reaction is to get defensive. It takes a special person to both be confident in their decisions and tempered enough to question them. Most people struggle with taking criticism because it harms their self-image.

Even if you change your course, even if you're changing direction, willpower means never quitting and not fleeing. When you refuse to engage with a dissenting opinion, you succumb to willpower's greatest enemy: pride.

Your pride should always be derived from your will, not the other way around. There are many people who refuse to admit their mistakes because of their pride, and pride is a very poor substitute for will because pride can be broken. If humiliation can break you, then your will was never strong in the first place. Your will was a façade. Real willpower comes internally. You should be proud of your perseverance, your ability to never quit when things get hard—not of the fact you are special and always right for some divine reason.

Willpower is something that needs to be regulated. Just as one regulates all other emotions through discipline. The Kaiser and my grandfather struggled with being too willful, but some have the opposite issue. Many young men are rightly worried they aren't willful enough and that harms their ability to assert themselves, especially when they are in the right. Willpower is not something that just exists or is intrinsic to one person. Willpower is a muscle that can be built.

A good example is from a Stanford researcher. Veronika Job authored a study in 2010 which suggests "willpower—the capacity to exert self-control—is a limited resource that is depleted after exertion." The current scientific literature suggests using your willpower now, without time to recharge after, means you will struggle to use it in the future. More interestingly, one can expand their pool of daily willpower because "psychologists have found that willpower is a lot like stress: It's not just a psychological experience, but a full-blown mind-body response. The stress response is a reaction to an external threat, for example a fire alarm going off. In contrast, the willpower response is a reaction to an internal conflict. You want to do one thing, such as smoke a cigarette or super-size your lunch, but know you shouldn't. Or you know you should do something, like file your taxes or go to the gym, but you'd rather do nothing" (Steakley, 2011). Because of its flexibility, willpower is something you can build through exercise and meditation.

I find it predictable my grandfather's willpower and his strength of character started waning in his old age because, as his body began falling apart, so did his impulse control. My grandfather's great vice was sugar. He was severely diabetic and suffered from multiple strokes. But he would still eat sugary fruits, candies, chocolates. He staved off decline through his impressive willpower, but as his willpower faded, so too did his physical health. He died at seventy-one, his decline in mental health swiftly following his body's degeneration.

While we can't expect all masculine people to develop his level of natural willpower, we can definitely increase it to a life-changing level and, unlike my grandfather, maintain that for longer. There are two things we can do to improve our willpower: exercise and meditation (Job, 2010).

Khabib Nurmagomedov is a paragon of finely-honed willpower. He is one of the most dominant fighters to ever live. He inherited the idea of weaponizing pace. Before him, Georges St-Pierre was infamous for pressuring his opponents with his jab and wrestling. Before Georges St-Pierre it was Randy Couture, and before Randy Couture, it was Dan Gable. This lineage of willpower as a tool is crucial to understanding the sport. Mixed Martial Arts is a space for humble learning. Current styles were built upon previous knowledge and the opportunity to learn from coaches, training partners, and even opponents is crucial for growth.

Another vital angle to understand Khabib is his faith. Aside from being an athlete, he's a devout Muslim. He uses prayer as a form of meditation, and it gives him strength. He will tell you, "Alhamdulillah; God gave me everything," when asked about his unshakable willpower (Sonnen, 2020).

One of the tenets of Islam is the salaat prayer, uttered five times a day. Performing the prayers gives Muslim adherents a static routine and time to meditate on their thoughts and to focus on one clear goal. Praying to Mecca isn't magical.

Praying itself isn't magical, either, but regular meditation has been clinically proven to create "changes [in] both the function and structure of the brain to support self-control. For example, regular meditators have more gray matter in the prefrontal cortex" (Steakley, 2011). The pre-frontal cortex is responsible for our executive functions like focus and logical thinking, both of which aid in the development of a willful mind.

Vices are dangerous because even their avoidance will keep you in a state of obsession. An alcoholic who quits cold turkey might spend too much of his time thinking about alcohol. The vice has still enslaved him without once touching his lips.

Moderation is the key. You can form a routine for yourself that helps you keep your vices in check. Sex, drugs, alcohol, sugar—all of these in excess are vices that will distract you from your goal. At the end of the day, willpower is the ability to forego instant gratification. Your willpower is the ability to follow a long-term goal.

Now the dark side of willpower is pride. And you have to learn to overcome that. The best way to deal with pride is to learn to admit defeat and strength. To do that, you can never quit. You have to keep going forward. You can never flee. You may have to retreat, but you never flee. Doing speech and debate in high school made me a very precocious and argumentative child in a community of other precocious and argumentative children, and debate has a work warding mechanism where you were rewarded with success and fame and even obsessive admiration. The most important skill I learned was learning to admit if I was wrong. It wasn't something that came naturally to me and was incredibly difficult, especially if I didn't like the person pointing a finger.

No one likes the taste of humble pie, but no one can deny its nutritional value. Learning to admit one's mistakes is a sign of growth and creates a base for future learning.

Suppose you don't admit when you're wrong. Suppose you're stubborn about your position, forever. In that case, it's going to be very hard for people to place their trust in your counsel. If your ideas never change with changing information, you're never going to be an arbiter of truth: you're never going to be truly, unfailingly reliable.

Highschool debate taught me the importance of strategy in conversation. If you are wrong then you must be the first to admit your flaws. Don't give your opponent the satisfaction of victory. No—instead, thank them. Tell them, "I see, I was wrong. I made an error in my calculations. Thank you for rectifying it. I am right now."

You win by changing your mind and accepting the new data. You didn't make it about your opponent's victory. You made it about your personal growth. You're not making it about them; you're replacing in the satisfaction of victory by giving yourself the satisfaction of growth. Suppose you can see defeat as an argument but frame it as your victory. You will never lose it.

Insults exist to break your will. When you demonstrate the principled fortitude and are willing to understand nuance, you can make adjustments wherever you are wrong. Anyone who's afraid of admitting they're wrong will be a failure as a leader. It takes strength of will to sacrifice one's ego to gain results. In the long run, that is the type of leader who changes the world.

Your willpower will be strengthened as you develop your strength, your exercise, your mental strength, your mental exercise. And as you find your weaknesses and eliminate them. If you're willing to be right, accepting your faults and fixing them makes you more right. I think the most important takeaway is you shouldn't be a Kaiser; you should be a king.

ACKNOWLEDGMENTS

—

This book was a challenging venture. Masculinity is not an objective phenomenon; it is a social construct, one that has many unique interpretations across cultural lines. It follows, therefore, when speaking about masculinity—when writing an entire book about it—it is enormously difficult to maintain subjectivity while providing wisdom that can apply to every form of masculine culture. Through this book, I hope to help young men and women understand masculinity and build upon it, and I would love to thank all those who aided in its production.

I'd like to acknowledge those who have given this book, and the stories within it, legs strong enough to stand on: **Edmaicon Moraes, Elan Biswas, Daniel Che, Chael Sonnen,** and **Matt Taibbi**.

I'd also like to gratefully acknowledge **Eric Koester, Grace Chen, Tina Zaman, Daniel Che, Suyash Jain, Ramya Sarangarajan, Soham Mukherjee, Nicholas Pinto, Raj Menon,** and **Elan Biswas** for their assistance in funding this book.

Lastly, I'd like to acknowledge a few sources of inspiration: **Ernest Hemingway, Oscar Wilde, Bernie Sanders, George Orwell, Sessue Hayakawa, Joe Biden**, and **my grandfather**. Each of these men represents a strong and healthy form of masculinity in their own way and, through this book, I hope their efforts at redefining such an essential pillar of society are also impressed upon you.

APPENDIX

INTRODUCTION

Bindel, Julie. "Obama's Right, Women Are Superior to Men. Let Me Count the Ways ... | Julie Bindel." *Guardian News and Media*, December 6, 2017. https://www.theguardian.com/commentisfree/2017/dec/06/obama-women-superior-men-washing-up-driving-patriarchy.

Crawford, Krysten. "New Stanford Education Study Shows Where Boys and Girls Do Better in Math, English." *Stanford Graduate School of Education*, July 18, 2019. https://ed.stanford.edu/news/new-stanford-education-study-shows-where-boys-and-girls-do-better-math-english

Kuper, Simon. "Why Are Boys Falling behind at School?" *Financial Times*, 14 Dec. 2018. www.ft.com/content/3b2509f2-fda2-11e8-aebf-99e208d3e521.

CHAPTER 1

Barbee, Jeff. "Africa's New Elite Force: Women Gunning for Poachers and Fighting for a Better Life." *The Guardian. Guardian News and Media*, December 17, 2017. https://www.theguardian.com/environment/2017/dec/17/poaching-wildlife-africa-conservation-women-barbee-zimbabwe-elephant-rhino

Crawford, Krysten. "New Stanford Education Study Shows Where Boys and Girls Do Better in Math, English." *Stanford Graduate School of Education*, July 18, 2019. https://ed.stanford.edu/news/new-stanford-education-study-shows-where-boys-and-girls-do-better-math-english

Farrell, Warren. 1993. *The myth of male power: why men are the disposable sex.* New York: Simon & Schuster.

Hall-Lande, Jennifer A., Maria E. Eisenberg, Sandra L. Christenson, and Dianne Neumark-Sztainer. "Social isolation, psychological health, and protective factors in adolescence." *Adolescence* 42, no. 166 (2007)

International Finance Corporation (IFC). "IFC jobs study assessing private sector contributions to job creation and poverty reduction: preliminary findings and conclusions." (2012).

Kearns, Megan C., Dennis E. Reidy, and Linda Anne Valle. "The role of alcohol policies in preventing intimate partner violence: A review of the literature." *Journal of Studies on Alcohol and Drugs* 76, no. 1 (2015): 21-30.

Ministry of Health, Labour and Welfare. Status of Suicide in 2019 [Japanese]. 2020. https://www.npa.go.jp/safetylife/seianki/jisatsu/R02/R01_jisatuno_joukyou.pdf (accessed October 23, 2020).

Salter, Michael. "The Problem With a Fight Against Toxic Masculinity." *The Atlantic. Atlantic Media Company*, June 19, 2020. https://www.theatlantic.com/health/archive/2019/02/toxic-masculinity-history/583411/

Semuels, Alana. "Poor Girls Are Leaving Their Brothers Behind." *The Atlantic. Atlantic Media Company*, November 27, 2017. https://www.theatlantic.com/business/archive/2017/11/gender-education-gap/546677/.

Ruch, D.A., et al. "Trends in Suicide Among Youth Aged 10 to 19 Years in the United States, 1975 to 2016." *JAMA Netw Open.* 2019; 2 (5):e193886. doi:10.1001/jamanetworkopen.2019.3886

Targum, S. D., and Junko Kitakana. (2012). "Overwork suicide in Japan: a national crisis." *Innovations in clinical neuroscience*, 9 (2), 35–38.

CHAPTER 2

Bardasi, Elena, and Mark P. Taylor. *Marriage and wages.* No. 2005-01. ISER Working Paper Series, 2005.

Broughton, J.M., Weitzel, E.M. "Population reconstructions for humans and megafauna suggest mixed causes for North American Pleistocene extinctions." *Nature Communications* 9, 5441 (2018). https://doi.org/10.1038/s41467-018-07897-1

Bryant, Alison L., and Marc A. Zimmerman. "Role models and psychosocial outcomes among African American adolescents." *Journal of Adolescent Research* 18, no. 1 (2003): 36-67.

Enfu Cheng, and Yexia Sun. "Israeli Kibbutz: A Successful Example of Collective Economy." *World Review of Political Economy* 6, no. 2 (2015): 160-75. Accessed March 5, 2021. doi:10.13169/worlrevipoliecon.6.2.0160.

Erik K. Olsen, The Relative Survival of Worker Cooperatives and Barriers to Their Creation, in Sharing Ownership, Profits, and Decision-Making in the 21st Century, 85 (vol. 14, Dec. 2013). http://community-wealth.org/sites/clone.community-wealth.org/files/downloads/article-olsen.pdf.

Khazan, Olga. "The Trouble With America's Water." *The Atlantic. Atlantic Media Company,* September 11, 2019.
https://www.theatlantic.com/health/archive/2019/09/millions-american-homes-have-lead-water/597826/.

Piliavin, Jane Allyn, and Erica Siegl. "Health benefits of volunteering in the Wisconsin longitudinal study." *Journal of Health and Social Behavior* 48, no. 4 (2007): 450-464.

Richarz, Allen. "In Japan's Vanishing Rural Towns, Newcomers are Wanted." *Bloomberg.com. Bloomberg.* Accessed March 5, 2021.
https://www.bloomberg.com/news/articles/2019-11-15/in-japan-s-vanishing-rural-towns-newcomers-wanted.

Semuels, Alana. "Highways Destroyed America's Cities." *The Atlantic. Atlantic Media Company,* November 25, 2015.
https://www.theatlantic.com/business/archive/2015/11/highways-destroyed-americas-cities/417789/.

Van Krieken, Robert. "Rethinking Cultural Genocide: Aboriginal Child Removal and Settler-Colonial State Formation." *Oceania* 75, no. 2 (2004): 125-51. Accessed March 5, 2021.
http://www.jstor.org/stable/40331967.

CHAPTER 3

Babcock, Linda, and Sara Laschever. *Women don't ask.* Princeton University Press, 2009.

Broughton, J.M., Weitzel, E.M. "Population reconstructions for humans and megafauna suggest mixed causes for North American Pleistocene extinctions." *Nature Communications* 9, 5441 (2018).
https://doi.org/10.1038/s41467-018-07897-

Carnegie, Dale. 1964. *How to Win Friends and Influence People.* New York: Simon and Schuster, 2007.

Hamstra, Melvyn RW. "'Big'en: Male leaders' height positively relates to followers' perception of charisma." *Personality and Individual Differences* 56 (2014): 190-192.

Matsudaira, Izumi, et al. "Parental praise correlates with posterior insular cortex gray matter volume in children and adolescents." *PLoS One* 11, no. 4 (2016): e0154220.

Mehrabian, Albert. *Nonverbal Communication.* Chicago: Aldine-Atherton, 1972.

Sugawara, Sho K., et al. "Social rewards enhance offline improvements in motor skill." *PLoS One* 7, no. 11 (2012): e48174.

CHAPTER 4

Berkowitz, Bill (15 August 2003). "'Cultural Marxism' Catching On". *Intelligence Report*. Southern Poverty Law Center. Archived from the original on 30 September 2018. Retrieved 2 October 2018.

Britannaca. "Gates Foundation." *Encyclopædia Britannica*. www.britannica.com/topic/Gates-Foundation.

Cheng, Maria. "Countries Urge Drug Companies to Share Vaccine Know-How." *AP NEWS, Associated Press*, 1 Mar. 2021, apnews.com/article/drug-companies-called-share-vaccine-info-22d92afbc3ea9ed519be007f8887bcf6.

Hancock, Jay. "They Pledged to Donate Rights to Their COVID Vaccine, Then Sold Them to Pharma." Kaiser Health News, 26 Aug. 2020, khn.org/news/rather-than-give-away-its-covid-vaccine-oxford-makes-a-deal-with-drugmaker/ (http://khn.org/news/rather-than-give-away-its-covid-vaccine-oxford-makes-a-deal-with-drugmaker/).

Mcleod, Saul. "The Milgram Shock Experiment." Milgram Experiment | Simply Psychology, 2017.
http://www.simplypsychology.org/milgram.html.

Piper, Kelsey. "Bill Gates's Efforts to Fight Coronavirus, Explained." *Vox*, 14 Apr. 2020, www.vox.com/future-perfect/2020/4/14/21215592/bill-gates-coronavirus-vaccines-treatments-billionaires.

Polet, Jeff. "Gates Admits Common Core Failure, Then Doubles down on It." *Philanthropy Daily*, 19 Mar. 2020, www.philanthropydaily.com/gates-philanthropy-failure-common-core/

Queally, Jon. "Bill Gates Says No to Sharing Vaccine Formulas with Global Poor to END PANDEMIC." *Salon*, 26 Apr. 2021, www.salon.com/2021/04/26/bill-gates-says-no-to-sharing-vaccine-formulas-with-global-poor-to-end-pandemic_partner/.

CHAPTER 5

Fresson, Megan, Thierry Meulemans, Benoit Dardenne, and Marie Geurten. "Overdiagnosis of ADHD in boys: Stereotype impact on neuropsychological assessment." *Applied Neuropsychology: Child* 8, no. 3 (2019): 231-245.

Greenblatt, Jeff. "How Space Technology Benefits the Earth." *The Space Review: How space technology benefits the Earth*, July 29, 2019.
https://www.thespacereview.com/article/3768/1.

Ludwig, Mike. "My Community Health Center Would Not Exist Without Bernie Sanders." *Jacobin*, 23 Jan. 2020, jacobinmag.com/2020/01/bernie-sanders-hillary-clinton-community-health-centers-crescentcare.

"Nikola Tesla." *Encyclopædia Britannica. Encyclopædia Britannica, inc.,* January 3, 2021.
https://www.britannica.com/biography/Nikola-Tesla.

Taibbi, Matt. "Inside the Horror Show That Is Congress." *Rolling Stone*. February 14, 2020. https://www.rollingstone.com/feature/inside-the-horror-show-that-is-congress-177955/.

CHAPTER 6

Arab, Arman, Sanaz Mehrabani, Sajjad Moradi, and Reza Amani. "The association between diet and mood: A systematic review of current literature." *Psychiatry Research* 271 (2019): 428-437.

Diekelmann, Susanne, Ines Wilhelm, and Jan Born. "The whats and whens of sleep-dependent memory consolidation." *Sleep Medicine Review* 13, no. 5 (2009): 309-321.

Duckworth, Angela L., and Martin EP Seligman. "Self-discipline outdoes IQ in predicting academic performance of adolescents." *Psychological Science* 16, no. 12 (2005): 939-944.

Duckworth, Angela Lee, Heidi Grant, Benjamin Loew, Gabriele Oettingen, and Peter M. Gollwitzer. "Self-regulation strategies improve self-discipline in adolescents: Benefits of mental contrasting and implementation intentions." *Educational Psychology* 31, no. 1 (2011): 17-26.

Gailliot, Matthew T., and Roy F. Baumeister. "The Physiology of Willpower: Linking Blood Glucose to Self-Control." *Personality and Social Psychology Review* 11, no. 4 (November 2007): 303-27. https://doi.org/10.1177/1088868307303030.

Job, Veronika, Carol S. Dweck, and Gregory M. Walton. "Ego depletion—Is it all in your head? Implicit theories about willpower affect self-regulation." *Psychological Science* 21, no. 11 (2010): 1686-1693.

Lin, Hause, Blair Saunders, Malte Friese, Nathan J. Evans, and Michael Inzlicht. "Strong effort manipulations reduce response caution: A preregistered reinvention of the ego-depletion paradigm." *Psychological Science* 31, no. 5 (2020): 531-547.

Mischel, Walter, Ozlem Ayduk, Marc G. Berman, B. J. Casey, Ian H. Gotlib, John Jonides, Ethan Kross et al. "'Willpower'over the life span: decomposing self-regulation." *Social, Cognitive, and Affective Neuroscience* 6, no. 2 (2011): 252-256.

Perkinson-Gloor, Nadine, Sakari Lemola, and Alexander Grob. "Sleep duration, positive attitude toward life, and academic achievement: the role of daytime tiredness, behavioral persistence, and school start times." *Journal of Adolescence* 36, no. 2 (2013): 311-318.

Sirikulchayanonta, Chutima, Wasoontara Ratanopas, Paradee Temcharoen, and Suwat Srisorrachatr. "Self discipline and obesity in Bangkok school children." *BMC Public Health* 11, no. 1 (2011): 1-8.

Stallone, Sylvester. 2006. Rocky Balboa. United States: Metro-Goldwyn-Mayer (MGM).

Tsapanou, Angeliki, Nikolaos Scarmeas, and Yaakov Stern. "Sleep and the aging brain: A multifaceted approach." *Sleep Science* 13, no. 2 (2020): 152.

CHAPTER 7

Choi, K. W., Zheutlin, A. B., Karlson, R. A., Wang, M. J., Dunn, E. C., Stein, M. B., Karlson, E. W., & Smoller, J. W. (2020). Physical activity offsets genetic risk for incident depression assessed via electronic health records in a biobank cohort study. *Depression and anxiety*, 37(2), 106–114. https://doi.org/10.1002/da.22967

Collins, Graham P. "Within Any Possible Universe, No Intellect Can Ever Know It All." *Scientific American*, March 1, 2009. https://www.scientificamerican.com/article/limits-on-human-comprehension/.

Floris Huider, et al., Major Depressive Disorder and Lifestyle: Correlated Genetic Effects in Extended Twin Pedigrees, *Genes*, 10.3390/genes12101509, **12**, 10, (1509), (2021).

Kraus, Nina, Jane Hornickel, Dana L. Strait, Jessica Slater, and Elaine Thompson. "Engagement in community music classes sparks neuroplasticity and language development in children from disadvantaged backgrounds." *Frontiers in Psychology* 5 (2014): 1403.

Metcalf, Gilbert and Qitong Wang. "Abandoned by Coal, Swallowed by Opioids." *Milken Institute Review*, April 23, 2020. https://www.milkenreview.org/articles/abandoned-by-coal-swallowed-by-opioids.

Moran, Aidan, Aymeric Guillot, Tadhg MacIntyre, and Christian Collet. "Re-imagining motor imagery: Building bridges between cognitive neuroscience and sport psychology." *British Journal of Psychology* 103, no. 2 (2012): 224-247.

Rasberry, Catherine N., et al. "The association between school-based physical activity, including physical education, and academic performance: a systematic review of the literature." *Preventive Medicine* 52 (2011): S10-S20.

Sale DG. Neural adaptation to resistance training. *Med Sci Sports Exerc.* 1988 Oct;20(5 Suppl):S135-45. doi: 10.1249/00005768-198810001-00009. PMID: 3057313.

CHAPTER 8

Angeloni, Cristian. "Rise of the TikTok Influencer-Adviser Worrying Financial Planners." *Portfolio Adviser*, January 22, 2021. https://portfolio-adviser.com/rise-of-the-tiktok-influencer-adviser-worrying-financial-planners/.

Allas, Tera, et al. "An Experiment to Inform Universal Basic Income." *McKinsey & Company*, 23 June 2021. www.mckinsey.com/industries/public-and-social-sector/our-insights/an-experiment-to-inform-universal-basic-income.

Ayres, Chris, and David Levesley. "The Truth about Dan Bilzerian." *British GQ*, July 19, 2017. https://www.gq-magazine.co.uk/article/the-truth-about-dan-bilzerian.

Carter, Shawn. "Over Half of Americans Delay or Don't Get Health Care Because They Can't Afford It-These 3 Treatments Get Put off Most." *CNBC*, 3 Apr. 2019. www.cnbc.com/2018/11/29/over-half-of-americans-delay-health-care-becasue-they-cant-afford-it.html.

Davies, Rob. "Does Robinhood Owe Too Much to Its Rich Backers?" *The Guardian*, January 30, 2021. https://www.theguardian.com/business/2021/jan/30/does-robinhood-owe-too-much-to-its-rich-backers.

Delis, Manthos, Iftekhar Hasan, Thomas To, and Eliza Wu. "The real effects of bank lobbying: Evidence from the corporate loan market." (2022)

Fortado, Lindsay. "Hedge Funds Start to Face up to Extreme Gender Imbalance." *Financial Times*, August 16, 2017. https://www.ft.com/content/2105675c-7eb3-11e7-ab01-a13271d1ee9c.

Hedgeweek Editors. "New Study Finds No Evidence of Outperformance by Hedge Fund 'Best Ideas'." *Hedgeweek*, May 4, 2020. https://www.hedgeweek.com/2020/05/04/285298/new-study-finds-no-evidence-outperformance-hedge-fund-best-ideas.

Hemmings, Chris. "Why Are Most Problem Gamblers Men?" *BBC News*, February 13, 2018. https://www.bbc.com/news/uk-43002380.

Jabr, Ferris. "How the Brain Gets Addicted to Gambling." *Scientific American*, November 1, 2013. https://www.scientificamerican.com/article/how-the-brain-gets-addicted-to-gambling/.

Roberts, Chris. "Dan Bilzerian Is A Renter, And Someone Else Pays His Credit Card Bills: Lawsuit." *Forbes Magazine*, July 13, 2020. https://www.forbes.com/sites/chrisroberts/2020/07/09/dan-bilzerian-is-a-renter/?sh=1fb98c007df5.

Stewart, Barbara. "The Equality Equation: Three Reasons Why the Gender Investing Gap Is Closing." *CFA Institute Enterprising Investor*, May 4, 2020. https://blogs.cfainstitute.org/investor/2019/05/22/the-equality-equation-three-reasons-why-the-gender-investing-gap-is-closing/.

Taibbi, Matt. "Why Isn't Wall Street in Jail?" *Rolling Stone*, 10 Feb. 2011. www.rollingstone.com/politics/politics-news/why-isnt-wall-street-in-jail-179414/.

Taylor, Chris. "Why Women Are Better Investors: Study." *Reuters*, June 7, 2017. https://www.reuters.com/article/us-money-investing-women/why-women-are-better-investors-study-idUSKBN18Y2D7.

Treisman, Rachel. "California Program Giving $500 No-Strings-Attached Stipends Pays Off, Study Finds." *NPR*, 4 Mar. 2021. www.npr.org/2021/03/04/973653719/california-program-giving-500-no-strings-attached-stipends-pays-off-study-finds.

Wilbermay, Charles K., et al. "The Casino Economy: How Wall Street Is Gambling with America's Financial Future." *America Magazine*, 9 Dec. 2012. www.americamagazine.org/issue/775/article/casino-economy.

Wong, Gloria, Nolan Zane, Anne Saw, and Alan Ka Ki Chan. "Examining Gender Differences for Gambling Engagement and Gambling Problems among Emerging Adults." *Journal of Gambling Studies* 2 (June 2013): 171-189. doi:10.1007/s10899-012-9305-1

CHAPTER 9

Abelman, Devon. "How K-Pop Stars Are Influencing Men in Korea to Get PlasticSurgery." *Allure.* Accessed January 3, 2021. https://www.allure.com/story/korean-men-plastic-surgery-trends.

Baudrillard, Jean, 1929-2007. *Simulacra and Simulation.* Ann Arbor :University of Michigan Press, *1994.*

Morris, Steven. "Up to a Million Britons Use Steroids for Looks Not Sport." *The Guardian. Guardian News and Media,* January 21, 2018. https://www.theguardian.com/society/2018/jan/21/up-to-a-million-britons-use-steroids-for-looks-not-sport.

Pesek, William. "BTS Can't SAVE South Korea, Though ITS $4.7 Billion GDP Boost Sounds Good." Forbes, Forbes Magazine, 10 Oct. 2019, www.forbes.com/sites/williampesek/2019/10/10/bts-cant-save-south-korea-though-its-47-billion-gdp-boost-sounds-good/?sh=24cf3c452412.

Phillipou, Andrea, and David Castle. "Body Dysmorphic Disorder in Men." *RACGP. The Royal Australian College of General Practitioners.* Accessed January 3, 2021. https://www.racgp.org.au/afp/2015/november/body-dysmorphic-disorder-in-men/.

Phillips, K. A., & Castle, D. J. (2001). Body dysmorphic disorder in men. *BMJ* (Clinical research ed.), 323(7320), 1015–1016. https://doi.org/10.1136/bmj.323.7320.1015

Tyson, Gareth & Perta, Vasile & Haddadi, Hamed & Seto, Michael. A First Look at User Activity on Tinder. 2016.

CHAPTER 10

Bueno Antoinette. "Inside Joe Biden's History of Heartbreaking Tragedy and Triumph." *Entertainment Tonight,* November 20, 2020. https://www.etonline.com/inside-joe-bidens-history-of-heartbreaking-tragedy-and-triumph-151904.

Contoyannis, Paul, and Nigel Rice. "The impact of health on wages: evidence from the British Household Panel Survey." *Empirical Economics* 26, no. 4 (2001): 599-622.

Felitti, Vincent J., Robert F. Anda, Dale Nordenberg, David F. Williamson, Alison M. Spitz, Valerie Edwards, and James S. Marks. "Relationship of childhood abuse and household dysfunction to many of the leading causes of death in adults: The Adverse Childhood Experiences (ACE) Study." *American Journal of Preventive Medicine* 14, no. 4 (1998): 245-258.

Levingston, Steven, et al. "Joe BIDEN: Life before the Presidency." *Miller Center,* 20 Jan. 2021, https://millercenter.org/joe-biden-life-presidency.

Linskey, Annie. "The Security Guard Blurted 'I Love You' to Joe Biden in an Elevator. One Viral Video Later, She Nominated Him for President." *The Washington Post*, August 19, 2020. https://www.washingtonpost.com/politics/the-security-guard-blurted-i-love-you-to-joe-biden-in-an-elevator-one-viral-video-later-she-will-nominate-him-for-president/2020/08/18/df652f04-e178-11ea-b69b-64f7b0477ed4_story.html.

McGann, Laura. "The Agonizing Story of Tara Reade." *Vox*, May 7, 2020. https://www.vox.com/2020/5/7/21248713/tara-reade-joe-biden-sexual-assault-accusation.

Schreckinger, Ben, Jeremy B. White, Sam Sutton and Carly Sitrin, and Bill Mahoney and Josh Gerstein. "Biden, Inc.: How 'Middle Class' Joe's Family Cashed in on the Family Name." *POLITICO Magazine*, August 2, 2019. https://www.politico.com/magazine/story/2019/08/02/joe-biden-investigation-hunter-brother-hedge-fund-money-2020-campaign-227407.

CHAPTER 11

Bagemihl, Bruce. *Biological Exuberance: Animal Homosexuality and Natural Diversity.* New York : St. Martin's Press. 1999. https://archive.org/details/biologicalexuber00bage/page/391/mode/2up

Chael Sonnen. "Khabib - GSP - Couture - Gable..." YouTube. December 16, 2020. Video, 10:03. https://www.youtube.com/watch?v=87kN1v2nlrA

Job, Veronika, Carol S. Dweck, and Gregory M. Walton. "Ego depletion—Is it all in your head? Implicit theories about willpower affect self-regulation." *Psychological science* 21, no. 11 (2010): 1686-1693.

Steakley, Lea. "The Science of Willpower." *Stanford Medicine*, 2011. https://scopeblog.stanford.edu/2011/12/29/a-conversation-about-the-science-of-willpower/

Made in the USA
Las Vegas, NV
27 December 2023